MAKE HEY!
while the sun shines

PIP LINCOLNE

hardie grant books

MELBOURNE · LONDON

8D

CONTENTS

Introduction

Oh my gosh! You picked up my book. That is so great of you! Thank you! I am Pip. This is my book. It is a book about craft and I am a crafty person. Maybe you are a crafty person too, or perhaps you are a nearly crafty person. Whichever you are, you have picked up the right book. If you are already a creative type, you may skip ahead and I will meet you on page 12. If you are itching to learn more about this thing called craft, then read on ...

Do you think that craft is not your style? You are wrong. Craft is even for a super-stylish person like yourself. There is no doubt that craft often gets put in a box marked 'old-fashioned' or 'shoddy' or 'incredibly floral', but it doesn't have to be like that. The kind of craft I like is rarely any of those things. The kind of craft I like references all sorts of things, from design, fashion and architecture, through to nostalgia, photography and happy holidays. The kind of craft I like is all about coming up with fresh ideas, while giving a nod to the things I love most. The kind of craft I like is like me. Perhaps the kind of craft YOU like is like you!

Do you think crafty stuff is just for people in brown sandals and prairie dresses? Wrong. Sandal-accompanied prairie dresses are nice and all, but crafting is also for people in polka-dotted frocks or long shorts or pleated skirts or skinny jeans ... track pants ... even slacks. Craft is not the domain of one type of person. Craft is for everyone. Not only do we learn new skills when we make things, we get to revel in our own crafty cleverness (regardless of pant length or prairie sensibility). What could be better than that?

Do you think craft stores are scary? Do you think you need some sort of Creative Person Licence to go inside?! Maybe you think those stores are the domain of people with jaunty berets or bejewelled sweaters? Well, I beg to differ. Those stores are chock full of interesting, crafty things that are not just for the jaunty or jewelly. Nope. They are also for people just like you and me. Yep. So go inside.

Art and craft stores are an amazing goldmine for the crafty and the new to craft. You would not even believe the kind of things they have tucked away. These stores, and the awesome people who work inside, are a really great springboard for all kinds of artsy, crafty adventures. Get among them! Trip up and down the aisles and become familiar with what's on offer: printing supplies, yarn, markers for all sorts of mediums, air-drying clay, cute fabrics, things to sculpt with, things to stick with, things to paint with or draw with or etch with or stitch with. It's a DIY nirvana. Go gather inspiration.

This book is full of projects and ideas and even nice things to cook. It's all about sunshiney fun stuff to make and things to put you in a dipping-your-toes-in-the-river-shady-picnic-popsicle kind of mood. You can make things just the way I have made them, if you would like, or you can unleash your crafty ninja and use the suggested materials to launch into your very own great ideas and projects. I bet you are just brim-full of ideas. So go to it and see what cute stuff you can come up with! (Prairie dresses are optional but picnics are NOT!)
xx Pip

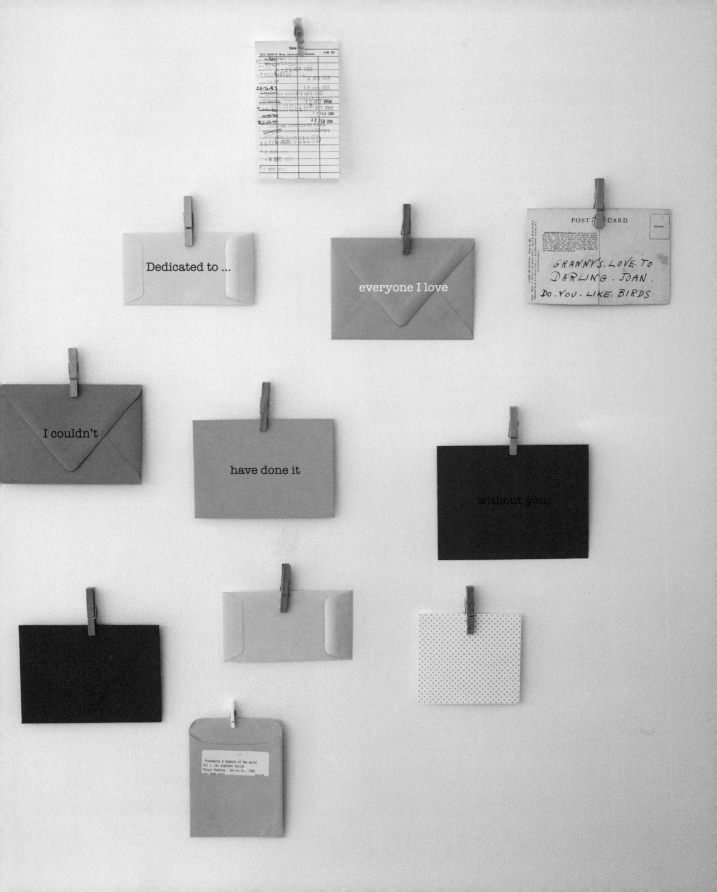

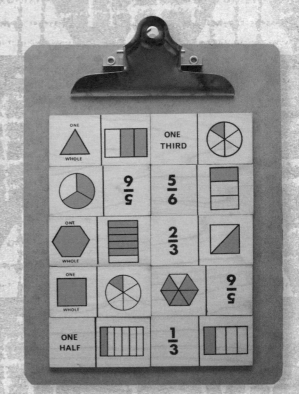

NICKEL PLATED RUST PROOF
PERFECT NEEDLES

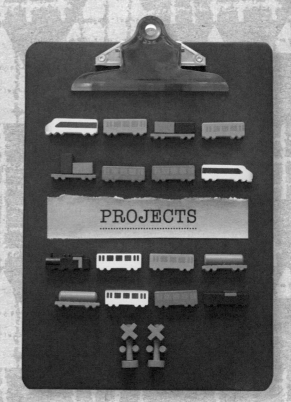

PROJECTS

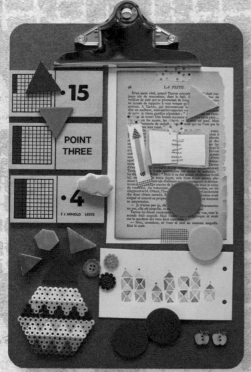

• 15

POINT
THREE

• 4

LA PETITE

CANBERRA
A.C.T.

GLENELG
S.A.

MELBOURNE
AUSTRALIA

SOUTH COAST
N.S.W.

BRISBANE

COOLANGATTA
TWEED HEADS

NEW SOUTH WALES

COOMA

O'REILLYS
GREEN
MOUNTAINS
QLD.

BUNDANOON
N.S.W.

ADELAIDE HILLS
S.A.

WELCOME FAMILY FLAG

I think it's a really great tradition to make a family flag. You can make one just like mine, or you can customise it a bit to make your flag truly your own. I don't think you can get a cheerier welcome than this! Cheerio! Off you go!

FABRIC DETAILS

Finished size: Approximately 95 cm x 60 cm [37½ inches x 24 inches].

Seam allowance: Seam allowance is 5 mm [¼ inch] unless otherwise stated.

Before you sew: Fabric should be washed, dried and pressed nicely before cutting and sewing. This will prevent fabric shrinkage and dyes running.

MATERIALS

> Red cotton fabric for backing: 1 m x 70 cm [39 inches x 28 inches]
> Neutral calico or quilter's muslin for front of flag: 85 cm x 50 cm [33½ inches x 20 inches]
> Fusible interfacing (I used Heat and Bond Lite): approximately 1 m x 50 cm [39 inches x 20 inches]
> Brightly coloured cotton fabric for shield: 25 cm x 30 cm [10 inches x 12 inches]
> Neutral calico or quilter's muslin for embroidered piece: 24 cm x 13 cm [9½ inches x 5 inches]
> Brightly coloured cotton fabric: 30 cm x 30 cm [12 inches x 12 inches] in each of three different colours for triangle appliqués
> Pompom trim – 1 m [39 inches] plus matching thread
> Fringed trim – 1 m [39 inches] plus matching thread
> Stranded embroidery floss in various colours

EQUIPMENT

> Sewing machine and thread to match your fabric
> Scissors
> Straight pins
> Rotary cutter, quilter's ruler and self-healing cutting mat
> Measuring tape
> Iron and ironing board
> Unpicker
> Transfer pencil
> Embroidery needle: a sharp, thin one with a large eye
> Optional: small (10 cm) [4 inch] embroidery hoop

Let's make it

Cutting it out

Trim your red backing fabric to a rectangle measuring 61 cm x 95 cm [24 inches x 37½ inches]. Trim your calico flag front fabric to a rectangle measuring 45 cm x 85 cm [18 inches x 33½ inches]. Trim your smaller calico piece (we will embroider it later) to 35 cm x 13 cm [13¾ inches x 5 inches].

1. Make the flag backing piece

First hem it! Hem the sides and the bottom edge of the backing piece. To do this, fold each edge in 5 mm [¼ inch] and press it with a hot iron so it's nice and flat. Fold the edge in once more, another 5 mm [¼ inch]. Press again, but this time pin it all into place. Now stitch the folded-over edge into place very close to the inner folded edge.

2. Make the casing at the top of the flag

With wrong side facing up, and the longer edges at top and bottom, fold the top raw edge down 5 mm [¼ inch] and press. Stitch into place. Press and snip all loose threads. Still with wrong side facing up, fold this top hemmed edge down a full 5 cm [2 inches]. Press and pin into place. Stitch a seam along the lower edge to create a casing. Stitch this seam once more for extra strength. Nice work! Go YOU! Your flag backing piece is neatly hemmed and your casing is done too! Let's move on.

3. Make the flag front piece

First hem it! Hem each side of the plain calico flag front panel. Do this by folding each edge in 5 mm [¼ inch] and pressing it with a hot iron so it's nice and flat. Fold the edge in once more, another 5 mm [¼ inch]. Press again, but this time pin it all into place. Now stitch the folded-over edge down very close to the folded inner edge, using matching thread. Trim your loose threads neatly and press the whole shebang once more. Nice work.

4. Transfer, cut out and appliqué (stitch!) the shield and triangles

Prepare the shapes first, using the templates in the pocket at the front of the book. Trace the triangle and shield templates onto the papery smooth side of your Heat and Bond. You will need to trace eight triangles and one shield. Cut the shapes out roughly (not on the line just yet). Decide how many triangles you want in each colour. We cut four blue, two gold and two magenta. Have your shield fabric ready too.

Next, working with one colour at a time, place your fabric wrong side up on the ironing board. Put the roughly cut-out, traced triangle shapes on top of the fabric, with their papery smooth side facing up. Press them onto the fabric with a medium-hot iron. Use firm presses (not backwards and forwards ironing motions) so that the shapes don't move. Be sure the edges are well stuck down. Now you need to cut around the shapes, this time right on the line. You'll have a shape with lovely fabric on the front (right side out) and paper on the back. Repeat for all your triangle shapes and your shield too.

Lay your hemmed and pressed calico flag front on your ironing board, making sure it is nice and straight. Peel the backing paper from the shield piece and carefully position it (nice and straight once more!) in the centre of the flag. Check our image to be doubly sure of your placement and then iron the piece on with a medium-hot iron and firm, quick presses. Iron the triangles into shape in the same manner, checking their position and alignment carefully before peeling and ironing on. Bravo!

5. Let's get fancy with our embroidery

Now you can go wild with a bit of embroidery. Using contrasting threads and a variety of stitches, embellish the edges of your appliquéd shapes with gay abandon. We used fly stitch, feather stitch, chain stitch, herringbone stitch and a starry stitch too. The more stitches the better, I say! It can be tricky to push the needle through the layers of adhesive and fabric, so take your time and drink tea and have lots of breaks to avoid frustration.

6. Welcome

Trace carefully over the 'welcome' template with a transfer pencil. Trim this traced-over piece about 1 cm [⅜ inch] from the edges of the text. Pin into place neatly in the very centre of the smaller calico piece. Be sure it's pinned away from the soon-to-be-hemmed edges of the calico, and that the pins are

in place around the text, not ON the text. Press the text part of the paper with a medium-hot iron to transfer the text. Well done! Now embroider over the lines with a neat backstitch. You can use an embroidery hoop if you like, but I didn't.

Press your work neatly on the reverse side, and trim any loose threads very close to the fabric. With the wrong side facing up, fold each edge in 5 mm [¼ inch]. Press the folded edges well with a hot iron. Position the embroidered piece on top of the shield. Pin and then stitch into place very close to the folded edge to secure.

7. Trim your flag

Pin your pompom trim along the top edge of the flag front, as shown in our photo. Stitch into place with matching thread. Pin the fringe trim along the bottom edge of the flag, as shown in our photo. Stitch into place with matching thread.

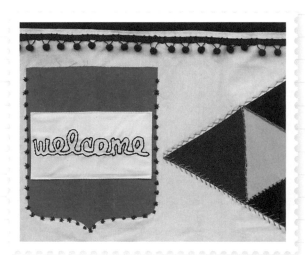

AMAZINGLY CUTE
GIFT BAGS

You will not believe how easy it is to carve your very own stamp. It honestly is. You will think you are an incredible crafty marvel when you have a go at this! It's a nice idea to make a whole stack of these bags at once, so you have nice hand-printed 'outfits' for your gifts to slip into! Your friends will think you are the cleverest ever and will demand presents all the time. But don't blame me for that!

MATERIALS

> Plain white paper
> Pencil
> Scissors
> Carving medium (such as 'e-z cut': available online or at art supply stores); or you can use a large white eraser if you can't find carving medium
> Bone folder or clean ruler
> An extra eraser
> Lino-cutting tool: one for making fine lines is good for beginners
> Small clean paintbrush
> Coloured stamp pads
> Hole punch

EQUIPMENT

> Paper bags
> String [twine]
> Coloured paper clips
> Mini pegs
> Colourful Japanese tape (washi)

1. Plan your design

Doodle around with your paper and pencil until you come up with a design that you like. With a sharp pencil, draw your final design onto plain paper, keeping in mind that it needs to fit on your carving medium. (If you like, trace around your carving medium onto the paper first so you know how much room you've got to play with.) Trim your paper design with a 1 cm [⅜ inch] gap around it. Flip your design over, so that it's pencil side down, and pop it atop your e-z cut.

2. Transfer your design

Use a bone folder or a clean ruler to transfer the outline, rubbing firmly against the wrong side of the paper and being careful not to move it around. Peek underneath to check that it's transferred nicely. If not, keep rubbing! If you make a mistake, use an eraser to rub it all out and start again. So really, there are no mistakes! Everything is fixable! (If you are super-confident you can draw straight onto the carving medium or eraser.)

3. Carve your design

Remove the paper and use your finest lino-cutting tool to carefully cut out the outline. Go slowly and carefully. You're carving away the excess, leaving the design part sticking up so that's what the ink adheres to. You only need to carve down a few millimetres [⅛ inch or so]. To get a clean, sharp line, it's best to apply slow but even pressure, rather than stopping and starting. Next, cut the excess away from around the outline. You can leave a teensy gap where you carved the outer part of your stamp's outline, or you can trim right back to the edge for a super-clean look. It's up to you. Brush any rubble away with a clean paintbrush. You are ready to stamp!

4. Stamp!

Ink up your stamp and test it out on some scrap paper. Are you happy with the result? You can always carve extra bits out, or neaten up lines now if you would like to.

Stamp your bag in any way you please. You could do a repeat pattern, or just a single impression. Do it the way YOU like! Let the ink dry.

5. Finish your bag

Punch a couple of holes in each side of the bag, thread your string [twine] through each pair of holes and knot the ends to create handles!

Variations

You could use this stamp to print your own wrapping paper or gift cards. You could make your own paper bags from scratch (find templates online!). You could also try printing with fabric paint onto some plain cotton fabric for ace DIY textiles! Be sure to heat set with a medium-hot iron if you are using fabric paint.

VERY WOOLLY FINGER PUPPETS

Puppets. They are scary to some people, but not to me. I am totally brave. I think you should face your fears and create the kind of puppet that you would want to hang out with. A bit smiley or spiky or smoochey ... whatever you like! This is a great project for the beginner knitter and these work well as decorations or party favours too!

MATERIALS

> Yarn: scraps will do, or a couple of balls of 8 ply [DK] yarn in your favourite colours
> Felt: again scraps are good, or several 10 cm x 10 cm [4 inch x 4 inch] squares of coloured felt for the details (trunks, ears, spikes, whatever!)
> Googly eyes

EQUIPMENT

> Scissors
> 4 mm [Size 6] knitting needles
> Wool needle
> Regular sewing needle and thread to match your felt scraps
> Hot glue gun and glue sticks
> Stranded embroidery floss

Let's make it

Cutting it out

First, you need to cut out your puppet's face details (ears, crown, antennae). Using our photo as a guide, simply hand draw the shapes onto the felt and cut them out. Or you can make up your own face designs!

1. Knit the basic finger puppet shape

> Cast on 15 stitches.

> Knit 20 rows.

> Cast off, leaving a long tail of yarn (about 30 cm [12 inches]).

2. Sew up and embellish your puppet

With the short end at the top, fold your knitted rectangle in half as shown in the diagram. Thread your yarn needle with the yarn tail. Sew neatly up the side and across the top with small stitches. Turn your puppet the right way out and carefully stitch and embroider details as shown! We have glued on the felt pieces and googly eyes with the hot glue gun. We also glued on a moustache and a crown. Ears and antennae can be stitched on with matching thread.

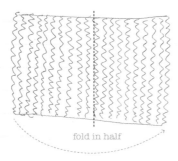

fold in half

Safety note

Please don't give these puppets to very small children, who might pull the glued-on bits off and swallow them. Embroider the details if you are giving these to small children.

Variations

You can go crazy adding stripes, scarves, horns, antennae ... the list goes on! You could make TEN of these, one for each finger or toe! You could theme them to storybook or fairy tales character, or to your favourite zoological species. You could use thinner yarn and finer needles to make these a bit tinier for very little fingers. You could knit a little pouch for them to hide inside!

VERY WOOLLY FINGER PUPPETS

SWEET RIDE BIKE SEAT COVER

Of course you need a fancy seat for your bike. Maybe you need a few? You can make these from pretty fabrics or you can use a plasticky fabric to keep things waterproof and easy to clean. Your bike will surely be the fanciest in town with a seat like this, don't you think?

FABRIC DETAILS

Finished size: Made to fit your bike seat.

Seam allowance: Seam allowance is 1 cm [⅜ inch] unless otherwise stated.

Before you sew: Fabric should be washed, dried and pressed nicely before cutting and sewing. This will prevent fabric shrinkage and dyes running. (Don't do this if your fabric is plasticised, or it will melt!)

MATERIALS

> 1 fat quarter of cotton patchwork fabric for the main bike seat piece
> 4 pieces of fabric for the sides, front and back of the seat: each measuring about 30 cm x 15 cm [12 inches x 6 inches]
> 50 cm [20 inches] of elastic 1.5 cm [⅝ inch] wide
> 60 cm [24 inches] of ribbon 3–4 cm [1¼–1½ inches] wide

EQUIPMENT

> Roll of baking paper or some sheets of newspaper
> Pen
> Scissors
> Sewing machine and thread to match your fabric

Let's make it

1. Make your pattern pieces

Trace your bike seat like this: Take a piece of baking paper newspaper (or newspaper) and a pen. Pop it atop your bike seat. Now, trace a seat-shaped line about 1.5 cm [⅝ inch] bigger than your actual seat. Make sure you form four distinct lines. It will look like a bigger version of your actual seat. Perfecto!

trace your seat

Once you have traced your bike seat piece, fold it in half lengthways and carefully cut along the lines you drew. Cutting the seat piece like this means that each side is identical and your pattern piece is symmetrical. Don't cut the piece any smaller when you are cutting it out, if anything make it a bit bigger (in the name of symmetry!). Good work.

fold

Next, place this traced bike seat piece onto some more baking paper or newspaper. You need to draft the side, front and back pieces next. First, draw a line 10 cm [4 inches] from each side point. Connect these lines (see diagram). You need two pieces like this. These are your side pieces. Now make a back piece by drawing a line extending 10 cm [4 inches] from each side of the back of the seat. Again connect these lines. This is your back piece. Finally make a small piece for the front of the seat in the same way.

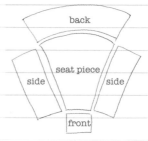

back

seat piece

side   side

front

2. Cut out your pieces

Lay each pattern piece onto your right-side-up chosen fabric and pin the pieces into place. Cut them out neatly. Remember you need one main piece, two side pieces, one front piece and one back piece.

3. Start sewing it all together

With right sides together, pin the front piece to the front edge of the main seat piece, matching the raw edges nicely. Stitch a 5 mm [¼ inch] seam. Stitch again for extra strength and snip loose threads.

With right sides together, pin one side piece to the side of the seat. Match the raw edges neatly. Stitch a 5 mm [¼ inch] seam. Stitch again and snip loose threads. Repeat for the other side piece, pinning and sewing it to the other side of the seat piece.

Finally match and pin the back piece to the back of the seat with right sides facing. Stitch a 5 mm [¼ inch] seam. Stitch again and snip loose threads.

4. Join the vertical seams

With your seat piece still the wrong way out, join your vertical seams by sewing up each matching pair. To do this, match the back pieces to the adjacent side pieces with their raw edges together. Pin and then stitch them into place with our trusty 5 mm [¼ inch] seam. Pinch in any excess at the top of the seam as you go. Stitch again for extra reinforcement. Repeat for the two seams at the front of the bike seat. Well done! We're getting somewhere now! Trim your loose threads and uneven edges and marvel at your weird floppy bike-seat-shaped piece.

5. Attach the elastic

Next, with the wrong side facing you, fold the outer edge up 5 mm [¼ inch] all the way around. Press well and pin into place. Stitch this edge down all the way around to secure. Trim your threads. Now, with the wrong side still facing upwards, fold your outer edge in 2.5 cm [1 inch] (all the way around once more). Pin and stitch into place 2 cm [¾ inch] from the edge you just folded over. Trim your loose threads and wonder if this will ever take shape. Now let's attach the elastic. This involves a bit of juggling. You need to stretch the elastic as you sew it in to place. Make sure you pull the elastic as tight as you can while you sew it down. Here is how: with the wrong side of your bike seat cover facing upwards, pin the end of the elastic to the centre of the back seat piece. The elastic should sit about 5 mm [¼ inch] from the folded edge so that it will be out of sight when it's all sewn up. Now, start to stitch it down with a line of stitching all the way around the lower edges of the seat cover. You need to pull the elastic as tightly as you can while you stitch so that it gathers the seat cover in nicely. Be sure that you are stitching it 5 mm [¼ inch] from the folded lower edge of your seat cover too. When you have sewn all the way around, reverse backwards and forwards with your sewing machine to keep things extra secure. Snip any excess elastic and loose threads. Sew this very same seam again, 5 mm [¼ inch] closer to the bottom folded edge. Be sure to keep your elastic stretched tightly as you sew.

6. Attach the ribbon for a snugger fit

Now we just need to sew the ribbon to the sides of your seat cover with three or four rows of stitches. Cut two pieces of ribbon each 30 cm [12 inches] long. Pin and sew them at the points shown in our diagram. Trim your loose threads and pop the cover over your bike seat. Tie up the ribbon for a super-neat fit, pop a baguette in your basket and off you go! Fancy-cute, no?!

Variations

Make your seat cover from a plastic fabric-backed tablecloth. Make it in a single fabric (Liberty print anyone?!) or in patchwork. Print your own cute fabric using hand-carved stamps (see page 16) or simple block printing!

VERY FUN PARTY BUNTING

Oh, bunting! Who would have thunk that colourful triangles could herald such festive times. Well they can. I know it. When I made this bunting a party started as soon as I hung it across the living room. It was called the 'I finished this bunting party'. You should have one too!

MATERIALS

> 3 m [3 yards] of ribbon 1 cm [⅜ inch] wide
> 1 ball (100 g) [4 ounces] of 8 ply [DK] yarn

Finished size: Triangles will measure about 14 cm [4½ inches] across the top and 14 cm [4½ inches] from top to tip. The bunting will measure about 2 m [2 yards] from end to end.

EQUIPMENT

> 3.5 mm [Size 4] crochet hook
> Tapestry or wool needle, with a nice big eye
> Scissors

Before you start: If you're new to crochet, see page 138. This book uses Australian and UK crochet terminology, with the US term in square brackets. For a full list of all crochet terms, see page 141. For this project you'll need to know how to do chain, slip stitch, double crochet (DC) and single crochet (SC).

Let's make it

1. Let's make the triangles first

Foundation row

Chain 3.

Row one

DC [SC] into second chain from hook. DC [SC] into next chain. Chain 1 and turn.

Row two

DC [SC] into first DC [SC]. DC [SC] twice into next DC [SC]. Chain 1 and turn.

Row three

DC [SC] into first DC [SC]. DC [SC] into second DC [SC]. DC [SC] twice into last DC [SC]. Turn at the end of the row.

The next 20 rows ...

Continue on with each row, using the following pattern. For every row:

> Chain up 1.
> DC [SC] once into the very first stitch of each row.
> DC [SC] once into every stitch along the length of the row.
> Lastly DC [SC] twice into the final stitch of every row. Turn at the end of the row.

You need to crochet 20 rows like this to complete the triangle. Your triangle will get longer and wider with every row. When you have crocheted 20 rows, fasten off securely, leaving a 20 cm [8 inch] tail. Now make your remaining triangles using the exact same steps!

2. Sew in your ends

You will have loose yarn ends dangling from each triangle. Let's get rid of those. Thread your yarn needle with the loose yarn end and carefully weave the end in and out of the stitches to conceal it. First weave it one way, then back the other way for

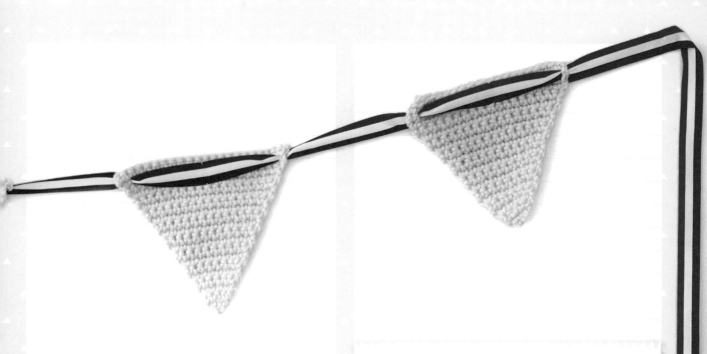

maximum security. You only need to go back and forth a couple of times. Next, snip the yarn very close to your work. If you give both sides of your triangle a little tug the snipped end will disappear within the stitches. Presto!

3. Join your triangles together

Thread your ribbon through the yarn needle and weave it in and out of the triangle pieces, making sure it doesn't twist (see the photo above). You can fold the ends of your ribbon over and stitch the raw edge under if you would like to, or you can leave it raw for a more rustic finish. Hang it up and break out the lemonade and the party cakes!

Variations

Vary the colours, making each triangle a different colour. Stitch a border all the way around each triangle. Embroider or cross-stitch text onto each triangle. By working more or fewer rows of DC [SC], make super-huge or super-tiny bunting using this method. Add some other stitches for variation or some fancy borders.

Safety note

Please don't hang this within reach of babies or small children.

BRONTE'S CUSHION

Inspired by the work of Maria Holmer Dahlgren and the amazing teensy squared quilts of the Quakers. Once you have made this cushion, you might even want to make your very own Quaker quilt. I probably won't as it might take a very long time. If you want to make a cushion, but not a patchwork one, skip to the end of this project to learn how to make a simple cushion cover.

FABRIC DETAILS

Finished size: Approximately 86 cm [34 inches] square. The patchwork piece will measure about 90 cm [35 inches] square before you sew it to the backing fabric.

Seam allowance: Important! When sewing this project, always use metric OR imperial measures; don't mix the two systems in the same project or you will end up with inaccurate seams. Seam allowance is 5 mm [¼ inch]: you need to stick to this religiously so that your squares will match up. Or you can use the lines marked on your sewing machine, or measure 5 mm [¼ inch] out from the needle of your machine and stick down a line of masking tape across the free arm of your machine to mark a guideline.

Before you sew: Fabric should be washed, dried and pressed before cutting and sewing. This will prevent shrinkage and dyes running.

MATERIALS

> Cotton patchwork fabric in various prints and colours: we need to cut 140 or so squares each 10 cm [4 inches] square. If you're using fat quarters (see page 128), buy ten of them for extra mix and matchability.
> Denim for cushion back: Two pieces each measuring 45 cm x 90 cm [18 inches x 35 inches]
> Cushion insert approximately 90 cm [35 inches] square
> Optional: 47 cm [18½ inch] square piece of unbleached calico or quilter's muslin to back your patchwork piece

EQUIPMENT

> Sewing machine and thread to match your fabric
> Scissors
> Straight pins
> Rotary cutter, 10 cm [4 inch]
> Measuring tape
> Iron and ironing board
> Unpicker
> Square plastic quilter's template and self-healing cutting mat

Let's make it

Cutting it out

First you need to cut out the pieces that make up the patchwork front of the cushion. Using your rotary cutter and template, cut out 10 cm [4 inch] squares. You will need about 140 (our panel is 10 squares by 10 squares; the remaining 40 squares are folded to give other shapes that are sewn onto the base squares). It's best to fold or stack your fabric into layers, so that you can cut several squares at a time. Make sure it's pressed neatly and each layer is smooth. Use a firm hand to hold your template in place and cut your squares with the rotary cutter using even, firm pressure. The rotary cutter does not work as well when only cutting one or two layers, so use that to your advantage and cut many squares at once! Speedy, no?!

1. Make up your squares

The triangle ones shown are made by folding a square on the diagonal and pressing it flat. Then you pin and top-stitch it into place on the diagonal on top of the square you want underneath it, being sure that your raw edges match up neatly. Both right sides should be facing up, and the folded diagonal edge should be sitting along the diagonal of the base square. You can machine top-stitch the triangles onto the squares for a speedy finish, or top-stitch them by hand if you want a portable project.

The larger rectangle ones are made by folding a square in half (edge to edge, not diagonally) and pressing it, then placing it on top of the base square and pinning, being sure that your raw edges match up neatly. Then top-stitch it to the base square. Both right sides should be facing up and the folded strip should run down the middle of the base square. Also sew along the raw edges to keep both patches together for when you sew them all up later.

The smaller rectangle ones are made by folding a square into thirds, with the raw edges concealed underneath, and pressing. Next place the small rectangle on top of the base square, being sure that your raw edges match up neatly. Pin and top-stitch into place near to the folded edges and along the raw edges too, to keep them together.

2. Plan your rows

Planning and careful sewing are the cornerstone of patchwork. So let's work row by row, and make sure each row is correct before moving on to the next. We need to be sewing ninjas now, taking our time, trying our best, sipping cool drinks and eating sandwiches. And we just need to try and sew a bit more slowly than usual for the best results. So, ninja, lay out your first row of ten squares in a sequence that you like. Maybe you don't want the same prints next to each other? Maybe you do? Make those kinds of decisions as you go. If you're not going to sew them all together in one session, pin them to a sheet or towel so you don't lose the sequence when you come back to it later.

3. Start sewing your first row together

Now take the first two squares of the row and put them right sides together. Pop a pin or two in to keep the edges lined up. Now sew a 5 mm [¼ inch] seam along the right-hand-side edge. Make sure the right sides of the fabric are facing each other, go slowly and keep that seam at 5 mm [¼ inch]. Open up the pair and snip the threads at each end. Take your next square and place it on top of the square on the right. Make sure the raw edges match on the right-hand side. Pin and stitch a careful 5 mm [¼ inch] seam again. Snip your threads again and continue on like this adding, pinning and sewing your squares with a 5 mm [¼ inch] seam. Check your seams. If any are a bit skinny, then re-stitch them a titch over

so that they DO measure 5 mm [¼ inch]. When you have ten nice squares all sewn neatly together, press the seams flat. Bravo!

4. Make your second patchwork row

You need to make your next strip now! Repeat the process above: arrange, match, pin, sew a 5 mm [¼ inch] seam until you have 10 squares. Now you have two completed rows (or strips!)

Place the two rows right sides together and match up all your seams. If we just go slowly, row by row, we can fix any mistakes as we go. (That said, mine certainly did not measure up super-perfectly, so don't beat yourself up.) If things aren't matching up, work out why. Maybe you made your seam the wrong width? You can easily correct any seams that are too wide or too narrow with an unpicker and a quick re-sew. Then things should be a bit better matched. And you will be more careful as you go along, because unpicking is a great deterrent!

5. Sew these two rows together

Pin at each square's seam, and at the beginning and end of the row to secure. Now sew 5 mm [¼ inch] seam all the way along to join the two rows. Snip all loose threads and press seams nice and flat to reduce bulk.

6. Make a third row

Construct your next row. Take the next 10 squares, then arrange, match, pin and sew them into a row.

Join this row to the previous row as we did before, correcting any too-big or too-small seams.

7. Keep going, row by row

Continue on making and stitching each row, one by one, until you have a square that is 10 rows by 10 rows. Trim, press and marvel at your work. Wowee! Have a break. At this point you can square up your patchwork piece so that all the edges are even. Your finished patchwork piece should measure 90 cm [35 inches] square. (Optional: You can also cut a piece of calico or quilter's muslin the exact same size as the patchwork piece and top-stitch it to the back of the patchwork. This will protect the back of your work and keep things neater.)

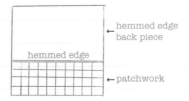

hemmed edge back piece

hemmed edge

patchwork

8. Make a simple cushion cover

Here is how to make a simple cushion cover. We are using the patchwork piece, but you could use any fabric for the cushion front! You can vary the size of the cushion too, once you are confident with this easy technique. (Your back pieces need to overlap at least 12 cm [5 inches].)

Take your two backing pieces and hem them like this: With wrong side up, fold the top edge down 1 cm [⅜ inch]. Press. Fold this edge down once more, this time by 2 cm [¾ inch]. Press and pin into place. Stitch a seam 1 cm [⅜ inch] from the folded edge to secure, removing the pins as you sew. Stitch a second line of stitching 5 mm [¼ inch] from the first line. Remove any stray pins, trim loose threads and press. Repeat with the other backing piece. Bravo!

Lay your cushion front piece (the patchwork piece!) right side up. Now lay one hemmed cushion back piece on top of it, right side down, with the raw edges lining up as shown.

the other hemmed back piece is underneath

↓ hemmed edge ↓

other hem →

Lay the other cushion back on top of that, again with the right side down and the raw edges matching. The two back pieces will overlap a bit in the middle.

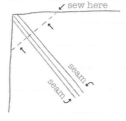

sew here

seam

seam

Pin into place around all the edges, using plenty of pins so things stay put. Stitch all the way around the square 1 cm [⅜ inch] from the raw edges. Stitch the same seam again for extra strength. Now trim your corners back and snip loose threads.

You can finish up here with a perfectly gorgeous cushion, or you can square the corners off. To square off your corners, your cushion cover needs to be the wrong way out. Flatten each corner out as shown in the diagram to form a triangular shape or point. Your seam will run down the middle of this point. Being sure that the seam on the bottom of your cushion is matching the seam on the top of your cushion, pin into place and carefully stitch a line 5 cm [2 inches] from the point as shown.

Turn your cover out the right way. Press it and squish your cushion inside. Now throw it on the floor and plant yourself on it, with something nice on the telly ... maybe *Downton Abbey*?

Variations

You don't have to make the patchwork version – you can just use a plain fabric panel for the front, or a cute print, or embroider a panel, or go for a speedy large-scale patchwork for the front panel. You could take the patchwork panel and use it as the basis for a quilt, too.

ENGLISH

in

ictuRes

STITCHERY by Virginia Tiffany

ttons

RIDE

A. LAMORISSE

**THE RED
BALLOON**

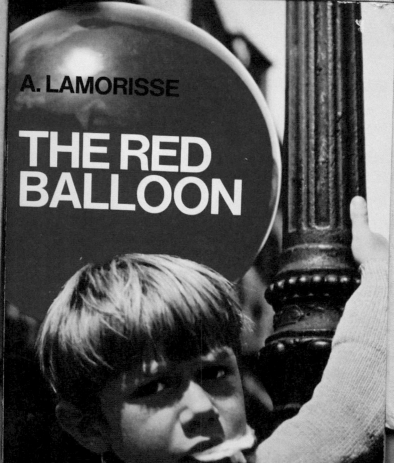

Alfred Könner

THE ROBBER

A Child's
GARDEN
of
VERSES

...ted by Alice and Martin Provensen

A GOLDEN PLEASURE BOOK

A Whitman BIG Tell-a-Tale

Toby
Tucker

by Jo Mendel

Kid Sister

by MARGARET EMBRY

TX 1199

CHATTY TOTE

Do you have something important to say? A custom slogan tote is just what you need to broadcast your message, isn't it? I thought so. This easy project shows you how to print text from your computer and transfer it to a fabric. You can then colour it in with markers (like I did) or even embroider it, if you are the super-fancy crafty kind!

MATERIALS

> Blank tote (buy one or make your own)

EQUIPMENT

> Microsoft Word (or any other word processing program with nice fonts)
> Blank white A4 paper and printer
> Embroidery transfer pencil and sharpener
> Iron and ironing board
> Pins
> Old newspaper
> Black laundry marker or fabric marker
> Pen and coloured felt-tip markers to practise colouring in with

Let's make it

1. Design your slogan

Create your slogan in your word processing program. Make sure it is nice and BIG and the letters are bold enough to trace easily. Run a test print and check it against your tote to make sure the size will be appropriate. If it's not, enlarge or reduce until you are happy with the result.

2. Print your slogan in reverse

Next, print your slogan onto blank paper in reverse. You can change your paper type to 'Transfer Paper' in your 'Print Properties' menu and it will print your text in reverse. Alternatively you can reverse the text in another image editing program or online at picnik.com.

If you don't reverse your slogan, it will end up backwards once you transfer it. So be sure you reverse that text! Once you have printed your reversed slogan, trace neatly over the text outline with the transfer pencil. This creates the basic text outline, which we will iron on in a minute!

3. Iron on your design

Next, press your tote nice and flat with a medium-hot iron. We don't want any bumps in the bottom layer messing up your slogan when you iron it on. Pin the paper with the traced text outline onto your tote bag right side down. The tracing needs to be against the fabric so you can iron on your slogan. Make sure your text is positioned nice and straight. Keep the pins well away from the area where your text is so they don't become obstacles to your iron. If you want to be absolutely sure the transfer doesn't move around, you could baste the design to the tote.

All smooth and pinned or basted? Start ironing your text outline on with a medium-hot iron using firm presses. (Pressing is what it says it is: put the iron down on one spot and leave it for a few seconds, then lift it straight up, put it down on another spot and repeat. Avoid making back-and-forth sweeping motions like you do when you're ironing, or your transfer might smudge!) Remove a pin and take a peek to be sure it's all transferred nicely, making sure you don't accidentally reposition the text. (If you do you'll get a messy transfer, so do this part slowly and carefully for best results.) When your outline is safely transferred onto your tote, remove the pins and marvel at your cleverness.

4. Colour in your design

Put many sheets of newspaper inside the bag to prevent your fabric marker from seeping through both layers. Make sure the newspaper is lying nice and flat so that you can draw and colour in without any lumps and bumps messing things up.

You can outline your text with the black laundry marker, drawing on the transferred line to conceal it and create impact. Now you can either colour in your outlined text with coloured fabric markers or with the black marker, or you can just leave it outlined – it's up to you! If you are not sure, practise on some blank paper and see which version you like best, then apply that look to your tote!

Variations

Use a fabric panel and embroider your slogan, then stitch it onto your tote. Try an image instead of text. Add some lace or ribbon to fancy things up, or a button-and-loop closure so you can button it closed. Use this idea in a more freehand way and simply draw or write straight onto your tote bag. Put your name on your tote!

GIRL'S BEST FRIEND PAPER WALL QUILT

This is a really beautiful, simple, portable project that will brighten up the gloomiest room. Or even the loveliest room. It's really the best thing for most rooms, actually. Please make it!

MATERIALS

> Several sheets of white cardboard: we used six large sheets
> Coloured paper: we used origami paper, but you could use giftwrap, wallpaper, vintage book pages, old maps or even fabric
> Thick cardboard
> Blu-Tack

EQUIPMENT

> Scissors (or craft knife if you have one, plus a metal ruler)
> Pen
> Tracing paper or baking paper
> Glue stick
> Ruler or bone folder
> Diamond template

Let's make it

1. Glue first

Let's glue the coloured paper (right side up!) to the cardboard first. Use the glue sparingly for a smooth finish. Use the edge of the ruler (or the bone folder, or indeed your fingertips!) to smooth out any air bubbles or bumps. Glue all of your pretty paper to your cardboard, making sure that it's as bump free as possible. The sturdy cardboard backing will keep your diamonds flat and ensure the edges don't curl up or tear.

2. Make your diamond template

Using the template in the pocket at the front of the book, trace the diamond shape onto the tracing paper. Cut out the diamond carefully and glue it to the thick cardboard. Now cut around the diamond, through the thick cardboard, to make a nice, sturdy final template. This will be super-easy for you to trace around.

3. Trace your diamonds

Pop your template onto your prepared sheets of cardboard and draw around the edges carefully with a marker. Trace as many diamonds as will fit on your card.

4. Cut your diamonds out

Probably best to do this in front of a nice DVD with a cup of tea, I think! Snip, snip, snip until you have a lovely stack of diamonds. Nice work! Make sure you have a few mini-breaks if you are getting a sore cutting hand!

5. Assemble your quilt

This is the best bit! Let's assemble our quilt of awesomeness! Use teensy bits of the Blu-Tack to attach your diamonds to your wall, pressing the shapes as flat to the wall as you can manage. It is best to arrange the shapes about 5 mm [¼ inch] apart to allow for any variations in shape: sometimes our cutting out is not super-precise, so leaving a gap between the diamonds means that any wayward geometry won't matter.

Variations

You could vary the shapes you use to make your wall quilt – triangles or squares or hexagons would be gorgeous! Make this as a long border that runs along your wall, rather than a central quilt shape. Instead of placing your shapes randomly, form a pattern!

FRIENDLY BLANKETS FOR COSY COUPLES

Two easy-peasy patchwork blankets designed to be together, but happy to be apart sometimes too. Make these for cousins or best friends or a cute couple. This is the perfect popcorn companion project, ideal for snuggling under with a cheesy movie or on a crisper picnicky evening! (Or you can just make one if you feel like some alone time.)

FABRIC DETAILS

Finished size: After you sew it all up, each blanket will measure about 50 cm x 1.5 m [20 inches x 59 inches]. And joined together they will be about 1 m x 1.5 m [40 inches x 59 inches].

Seam allowance: Seam allowance is 5 mm [¼ inch] unless otherwise stated.

Before you sew: Fabric should be washed, dried and pressed nicely before cutting and sewing. This will prevent fabric shrinkage and dyes running.

MATERIALS

> Twenty-four strips of 100 per cent cotton fabric, each measuring 13.5 cm x 53.5 cm [5¼ inches x 21 inches]. It's a good idea to use lots of different fabrics – the more variation, the better! If you would like to use just 12 different fabrics, you will need 12 pieces of fabric, each measuring 30 cm x 55 cm [12 inches x 22 inches]. Then you will need to trim them to the correct size (as detailed above)

EQUIPMENT

> Sewing machine and thread to match your fabric
> Scissors
> Straight pins
> Rotary cutter, quilter's ruler and self-healing cutting mat
> Measuring tape
> Iron and ironing board
> Needle
> Unpicker
> Four 1 cm [⅜ inch] wide sew-on metal press studs

Let's make it

1. Sort out your coloured strips

Each blanket is made up of 12 strips, so sort your strips into two piles of 12.

Let's make the top for the first blanket: Take one pile of 12 strips and on a clean, clear work surface arrange them as shown, matching their longest edges and making sure that they are in a nice random order. We are working out the placement of the fabrics, because you don't want two identical strips next to each other.

arrange your strips →

2. Start sewing

Now we need to sew the first two strips together along their longest edge: Off you go! Take the first two strips and place them together with their right sides facing and the raw edges even. You will only be able to see the wrong side of the fabric, right? Now pin their long edges together to keep things neat and easy to manage. Stitch along this longest pinned-together edge, from one end to the other, using a 5 mm [¼ inch] seam allowance. You will now have a pair of strips sewn nicely together.

Sew another strip to the first two. Grab the next strip from your pile and again with right sides facing, match the longest edges and pin together neatly. Then stitch along the pinned, matched edge with a 5 mm [¼ inch] seam allowance just as you did previously.

Sew the rest of the strips to the first three in the same way, sewing each strip to the last until you have 12 strips all stitched together like this. Yay for you! Trim any loose threads and press your seams nice and flat so that they will be easy to sew together. This is the beginning of your blanket top.

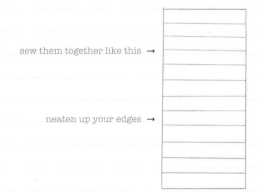

sew them together like this →

neaten up your edges →

3. Square things up

It's a good idea to 'square up' all your edges now. This will help you to match the edges and sew it all together easily. The best way to square up is to fold your blanket top in half and then in half again. You will end up with a messy-edged rectangle a quarter the size of your finished blanket top. Line up the folded edges with the lines on your cutting mat. They need to be butted up neatly against the lines on the mat. We don't cut the folded edges, we need to just trim the raw edges. So do that – trim the two raw edges of your blanket top to make them neat and straight. Use the lines on your cutting mat as a guide.

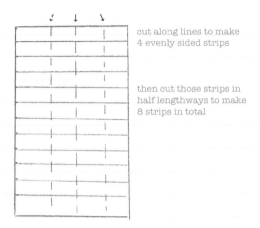

cut along lines to make 4 evenly sided strips

then cut those strips in half lengthways to make 8 strips in total

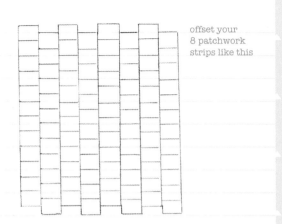

offset your 8 patchwork strips like this

4. Cut your patchwork rectangle into strips once more

Open it all up again and marvel at your neatened rectangle. Well done. Now we are going to cut this rectangle into four nice even strips (see the diagram above). Each of these four strips needs to be cut in half lengthways. Press all the seams nice and flat so they are easy to sew together.

5. Arrange your patchwork strips

Now you have eight patched strips. They are all the same width and length and are all ready to pin and stitch together. You need to organise them in an offset arrangement, as shown in the diagram. Try to keep like fabrics away from each other, and notice that the stitched seams between your patches don't line up. I know this seems wacky, but it will all work out. It's called the 'cut and stagger' method.

6. Stitch the first two strips together

Once you have organised your strips in an offset arrangement, take strips one and two and pin them together (still offset!) with their right sides facing. Only your long edge will match. The short edges will be uneven. Stitch them together with a 5 mm [¼ inch] seam allowance.

7. Stitch the next strip to the first two

Take the next strip and pin it (again offset) so that the long edges match, the right sides are facing and the short edge is kind of level with the short edge of the very first patched strip. Stitch a 5 mm [¼ inch] seam down the matched long edges.

8. Keep stitching strips

Continue pinning each patched strip to the last, being sure that each strip is offset, the right sides are facing and the long edges are matched. You will end up with a staggered-edged, lovely patched blanket top. Trim your loose threads.

9. Make the second blanket top next

Repeat these steps with the other pile of 12 strips, to make a second blanket top. Press your blanket tops.

10. Trim both blanket tops

Now we need to trim them so that they are squared up and the same size. Press both tops well and place them on top of one another, right sides up, matching the edges as best you can. Then fold this double layer into four and square up the raw edges, just as you did before.

11. Cut your blanket bottoms

Measure the size of the blanket tops and trim your two squares of calico to the same size.

12. Assemble the first blanket

Place the first patched rectangle right side up, smoothing it out neatly so there are no bumps or creases. Now place a calico rectangle on top of it, right side facing down. (Sometimes calico has a shiny side – that is the wrong side.) Match all your edges nicely and pin along both long sides and only one short side. Stitch around these three sides with a 5 mm [¼ inch] seam allowance, leaving one short side open. Repeat for the other blanket top.

13. Turn the blankets out and finish

Turn each top the right way out. Push the top corners out carefully and press the whole kit and caboodle nice and flat. Trim your loose threads. Now you need to finish the bottom edge. Tuck the raw edges in and press so that each folded and tucked-in edge is neatly matched. Pin and stitch to finish each blanket bottom neatly. Press and then trim those loose threads once more!

14. Attach your press studs

Match your blankets, side by side, along their long sides. Mark the points where you want to stitch your press studs on. Pull the studs apart and stitch each half firmly into position, one side on each blanket, double checking that they match up nicely before stitching. Snap your studs together, trim any loose threads and press your blankets neatly. Now make sure you give them to two VERY adorable people! These blankies will soften with age and become extra cosy and special.

Variations

You could make a super quick non-patchwork version of these with some cute printed fabric. You could make much larger scale patches for a faster result. You could make BOTH sides patchwork!

I HEART YOU NECKLACE

There is something cosy cute about a crocheted necklace. It's a little bit nanna and a little bit now. Make this for yourself or someone you are very fond of! You could even make a matching brooch or some loved-up earrings of the dangly persuasion. Or keep adding hearts and make the most romantic scarf you have ever seen!

MATERIALS

> Scraps of colourful 8 ply [DK] yarn: you can buy whole balls or just use oddments you might have already
> Two triangular jump rings: we used 2 cm [¾ inch] ones
> A length of chain to suit: we used 50 cm [20 inches] of nickel chain. Make sure your chain links are big enough to thread your jump ring through

EQUIPMENT

> 4 mm [Size 5] crochet hook
> Scissors
> Yarn needle
> Pliers

Before you start: If you're new to crochet, see page 138. This book uses Australian and UK crochet terminology, with the US term in square brackets. For a full list of all crochet terms, see page 141. For this project you'll need to know how to do chain, slip stitch and treble [double crochet].

I HEART YOU NECKLACE

1. Make six heart motifs in different colours like this

> Make a slip knot, leaving a long tail of yarn (about 30 cm [12 inches]). Put your slip knot onto your crochet hook and pull it firmly (but not tightly).

> Chain 5 stitches. Slip stitch into the very first stitch to form a ring. We are going to crochet into this ring in a minute!

> Chain 3.

> Now treble [double crochet] 10 times into the ring.

> We've almost made a round, but not quite. We aren't going to close this almost-round, either. The missing wedge at the top helps to form the heart shape.

> Fasten off to finish the heart and then snip your loose yarn, leaving a 30 cm [12 inch] tail. Pull the heart into shape, giving the bottom a tug to make it pointier!

Make your other five hearts in the same way, leaving those all-important long tails. The tails will help us to stitch the hearts into formation once we are ready.

2. Sew your hearts together

Arrange your hearts in formation, so that they resemble our photo. Take your first heart in your hand (!). Thread the uppermost yarn tail of this heart through your yarn needle. Carefully stitch each heart to the next with 3 or 4 well-hidden stitches, then weave the needle through the stitches of your heart to conceal some of the excess tail. Snip the tail off very close to your work. Repeat with the other hearts and tails, stitching them together and weaving in any loose ends.

3. Attach your jump rings and chain

Use the pliers to open up the jump rings and carefully hook them evenly onto each side of the crocheted piece. Thread the chain onto each jump ring. Now use the pliers to close them up again. Ta-dah! You made a necklace!

▼▼▼▼▼▼▼▼▼▼▼▼▼▼▼▼▼▼▼▼▼▼▼▼▼▼▼▼

Variations

Add one more treble [double crochet] to each motif to form a round and then slip stitch to close, then you can make this necklace from cute circles, instead of hearts! Make lots more hearts and stitch them together to form a scarf or a bracelet!

SUMMER CAMP WALL POCKETS

Maybe you could take this down to the shack and hang it on the back of the bathroom door?! All the cousins can stow their toothbrushes and shampoos and things in it. Or hang this in your bathroom and pretend it's summer camp every single day.

FABRIC DETAILS

Finished size: 70 cm x 1 m [28 inches x 40 inches].

Seam allowance: Seam allowance is 1 cm [⅜ inch] unless otherwise stated.

Before you sew: Fabric should be washed, dried and pressed nicely before cutting and sewing. This will prevent fabric shrinkage and dyes running.

MATERIALS

> 2.5 m x 70 cm [100 inches x 28 inches] of unbleached calico for the organiser
> Three pieces of unbleached calico each measuring 40 cm x 70 cm [16 inches x 28 inches] for the pockets
> Colourful fabric scraps for the tents: I suggest using five colours and you'll need 50 cm x 50 cm [20 inches x 20 inches] of each colour
> Scraps of various fabrics for the trees and bear – green: 30 cm x 30 cm [12 inches x 12 inches]; brown: 20 cm x 20 cm [8 inches x 8 inches]; grey: 10 cm x 10 cm [4 inches x 4 inches]
> Double-sided fusible interfacing
> About 3 metres [3 yards] bias binding at least 2.5 cm [1 inch] wide
> Piece of dowel measuring 70 cm [27 inches] (with a circumference of 2 cm [¾ inch] or less)
> Heavy string [twine] for hanging

EQUIPMENT

> Sewing machine and thread to match your fabric
> Scissors
> Straight pins
> Measuring tape
> Iron and ironing board
> Air-fading marker
> Pencil
> Scrap paper
> Glue stick
> Thickish cardboard [card stock]
> Drawing pins

Let's make it

1. Prepare the calico backing

Fold the large piece of calico in half widthways to make a rectangle 1.25 m x 70 cm [50 inches x 28 inches]. Make sure the folded edge is at the top.

2. Draw lines to mark where the bottom edges of your three pockets will sit

Using your fading marker, draw lines like this:
> One 1.5 cm [⅝ inch] from the bottom edge
> One 33 cm [13 inches] from the bottom edge
> One 64 cm [25 inches] from the bottom edge

3. Prepare your pockets

You will have a long rectangle with the fold as the top of the pocket. To neaten the bottom of the pocket, fold the bottom matching raw edges up 1 cm [½ inch] and press well. Quickly pop some pins along the pressed in bottom fold to keep things in place, then stitch 5 mm [¼ inch] from this pinned down edge to secure. We are just preparing the pockets at this point, we'll stitch them into place after we have added the triangle tents.

4. Make the triangle tents

Get the triangle templates out of the pocket at the front of the book and trace each one onto a small piece of regular paper. Cut them out roughly, then glue them to some thickish cardboard with your glue stick. Cut around them super-neatly to make your final template.

Now you need to trace these shapes onto the shiny, papery side of your double-sided fusible interfacing. Place the triangle on the papery side of the interfacing and simply draw around it with a pencil or pen. Don't draw on the bumpy side! You need to trace eight big triangles and eight small triangles. Next, cut the triangles out roughly: don't cut right on the traced line (yet!).

Cut your colourful fabric pieces a bit bigger (roughly again!) than the triangle pieces. Take each colourful piece of fabric and place it on your ironing board with the wrong side facing up. Place the roughly cut traced triangle of double-sided fusible interfacing on top of the fabric with the rough side down! Make sure it fits nicely. Remember, the rough side (that's the side with the glue on it) must be facing down! Press carefully with a hot iron to fuse – it will take several seconds to fuse the glue to the fabric, so check that it's all stuck down perfectly. It is? Perfecto! Now you need to fuse all the triangles to the various colourful fabrics: fabric wrong side up, double-sided interfacing bumpy side down for each one.

Are you done with that? You should have eight large, papery, fused fabric triangles and also eight smaller ones. Well done!

Fuse the small triangle to the larger triangle by peeling the papery backing from the small triangle. You will reveal a plasticky kind of coating where the paper once was. Place the triangle into position on top of the larger triangle. The plasticky gluey side is facing down. The right side of the larger triangle is facing up. Press into place. Do this with the other seven large and small triangles, mixing your colours up nicely.

Stitch the door details like this, using a straight stitch and your trusty sewing machine. Repeat for all the tents.

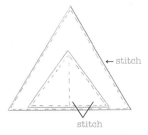

Trace and cut out the bear and tree templates in the same way, from the brown, green and grey fabrics. Put them aside to iron on later.

5. Sew on the tents and pockets

Fuse the tents to the pockets following the diagram opposite. Place them neatly and evenly as in the diagram, or a bit more randomly if you prefer. Be sure that they are away from the edges of the calico backing piece, though, so we don't lose them in the binding later! Then stitch the edges of the tents down too, for extra durability.

Place the pockets (with their finished tents!) in place along the lines you marked earlier. Make sure they are straight. Measure the distance from the bottom (or top!) edge at each end to be sure they

are even. Pin well and stitch 5 mm [¼ inch] from the bottom of the pocket again. Stitch the sides of the pockets very close to the edge to hold in place. We'll be covering this stitching later with our binding.

Once you have all your pockets stitched into place, you can add your compartments. Check the diagram to see where we put ours, or customise them: rule lines with your air-fading marker where you want the compartments to be, then sew along these lines, being sure to reinforce the stitching at the top and bottom so the compartments are nice and secure. Add your trees and bear by peeling the backing paper from them, putting them plasticky side down and pressing into place, then stitching around them, like you did before. Neaten up the side seams so they are all nice and straight and ready to bind.

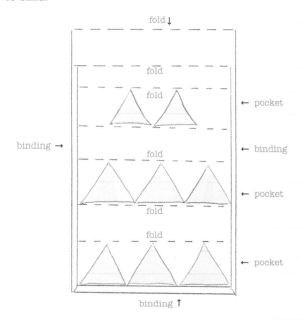

6. Bind your edges

Take your bias binding and match the raw edge to the raw side edge on the front of your organiser. Fold under about 1 cm [½ inch] of binding at the top, for neatness, then stitch along the fold in the binding to secure, all the way from the top to the bottom along one edge. Cut off the excess binding when you get to the bottom (you don't need to neaten it the way you did at the top, as it will be concealed by the binding along the bottom edge). Now fold the binding over to conceal the raw edges. Hand stitch into place using teensy stitches and matching thread on the back of the organiser.

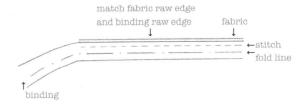

match fabric raw edge
and binding raw edge   fabric

←stitch
←fold line

binding

Repeat on the other long edge of the organiser. For the bottom edge of the organiser, you do the same thing, but before you sew the binding on, you need to fold under about 1 cm [½ inch] or so of the binding at each end to neaten the whole shebang. You don't need to bind the top edge of the organiser.

7. Make a casing for the rod to go through

Fold the top (folded and unbound) edge down 10 cm [4 inches] and press. Pin to secure and stitch into place 5 mm [¼ inch] from the bottom edge. This forms the casing for the rod hanger.

Put your dowel through the casing and pull it through so that it's even and straight. There should be excess on each end. Take a 90 cm [35 inch] length of string [twine] and tie a small, very firm loop at each end. Knot it a few times for extra strength and then pin to each end of the dowel with a drawing pin. Double check that it is securely fastened and then hang it up!

Variations

You could totally simplify this design and pare down the appliqué. Or you could make it even busier and add some embroidery, other forest friends or extra pockets to suit the things you want to stow inside!

SUMMER CAMP WALL POCKETS
67

MIX-TAPE À LA PIP

Of course you don't want to use regular sticky tape, because you are MUCH cuter than that. You are the type of person who asks for more, aren't you? You want your tape to deliver adorable surprises at every turn, don't you? Here is how to make unique and lovely tape with which to adorn presents for unique and lovely people.

MATERIALS

> Double-sided sticky tape, 2.5 cm [1 inch] wide
> Cute printed fabric scraps, or plain fabric scraps if you want to embroider or illustrate your tape
> For ten 30 cm [12 inch] lengths of tape, your initial fabric piece should be at least 30 cm [12 inches] long and about 40 cm [16 inches] wide

EQUIPMENT

> For embroidered tape: air-fading marker, needle and stranded embroidery floss; or sewing machine and thread in a colour you like
> For illustrated tape: fabric markers or a black laundry marker
> Scissors
> Rotary cutter, quilter's ruler and cutting mat
> Iron and ironing board
> Ruler and pencil

Let's make it

1. Prepare your fabric

Press your right-side-up fabric nice and flat and let it cool.

2. Embroider

Are you going to embroider? Now is the time to do that. Firstly, use your air-fading marker to rule lines at 4 cm [1½ inch] intervals across the width of your fabric. We are allowing a bit of extra fabric on either side to make things easier later on, so take that into account and don't embroider areas which will later be trimmed. Draw your design straight onto the fabric with the air-fading marker and stitch over it. Simple is best, because you don't want to be there all day, right? I mean, it's just TAPE!

It's best to separate the embroidery floss down to just a couple of strands before you stitch over your design. This will keep your stitched line nice and fine. You could also just stitch freehand using some of the stitches from our Stitch Library on page 118 (or others that you like!). Once you are done, cut along the lines you ruled, using a rotary cutter, quilter's ruler and cutting mat. You'll be left with embroidered strips slightly wider than the double-sided tape. Snip any loose threads to avoid too many lumps and bumps in your tape. We'll stick and then trim things up in steps 5 and 6.

You could also embroider the tape using the basic embroidery stitches on a sewing machine. If you want to do this, use a fresh new needle for the project, and replace it before you sew fabric with the machine again (because sewing through tape will make the needle blunt). If the needle gets gummy, remove it, wipe it with warm soapy water, then replace it and continue sewing.

3. Illustrate

Are you going to illustrate? Again, use your air-fading marker to rule lines at 4 cm [1½ inch] intervals across the width of your fabric. Then use your fabric markers to draw directly onto the fabric. You could do some practice sketches first if you are a bit nervous, or you can just dive in! Keep in mind that the fabric will be trimmed back to the width of your tape, so don't make your design larger than the 2.5 cm (1 inch) width. Once you are done, cut along the lines you ruled using a rotary cutter and quilter's ruler. You'll be left with illustrated strips slightly wider than the double-sided tape.

4. Simple fabric tape

Are you just going to use cute fabric and not get fancy? That is great too! There's no need to rule or cut. Just make sure your fabric is pressed nice and flat! Easy, no?

5. Assemble the tape (for embroidered, illustrated or fabric tape)

Cut your double-sided tape into 30 cm [12 inch] lengths. Lay your fabric (embroidered, illustrated or otherwise!) out neatly with its right side facing down.

Peel off the backing tape and press your tape smoothly against the wrong side of your fabric. Be especially careful to line the tape up nice and straight on the embroidered or illustrated pieces. You can juggle this yourself or recruit a friend to hold your fabric strips in place for you, while you wield the tape. It might help to tape the fabric to the table first, to stop it moving around, especially if you are doing this solo.

6. Trim things up

Next, simply trim your fabric lengths to the same width and length as your tape, using the rotary cutter and quilter's ruler. Cut your tape into 10 cm [4 inch] lengths and package up an assortment as gifts, or cut to size as you need it! Quick, go wrap something up! You are now a Wrapasaurus-Rex!

Variations

Make a super-fast version with ribbon or lace trim. Get some small people to draw on the tape for a very adorable kid-made effect. Try this with vintage book pages instead of fabric!

ABCD

abcdefghijklm

JKL

abcdefghijklm

RST

abcdefghijklm

XYZ

E F G H
pqrstuvwxyz
N O P
pqrstuvwxyz
U W
pqrstuvwxyz

PIGGY-BACK POCKET MONKEY

This monkey is an excellent best buddy to a child you know. His long arms are ready to wrap around someone's middle and tie in a bow. He will peep over their shoulder as they run through the park, and he has a pocket to stow secret stuff they might find. You can't get a better buddy than that, can you?

FABRIC DETAILS

Finished size: The torso will measure about 40 cm x 20 cm [16 inches x 8 inches] when sewn up.

Seam allowance: Seam allowance is 5 mm [¼ inch] unless otherwise stated.

Before you sew: Fabric should be washed, dried and pressed nicely before cutting and sewing. This will prevent fabric shrinkage and dyes running.

MATERIALS

> 30 cm x 110 cm [12 inches x 43 inches] of unbleached calico or quilter's muslin for the monkey face and body
> 1 m x 1 m [39 inches x 39 inches] of brown medium-weight 100 per cent cotton for the arms, legs, tail and features.
> 30 cm x 30 cm [12 inches x 12 inches] of double-sided fusible interfacing: we used Thermoweb
> Heat and Bond for ironing on the triangles and face patches
> Two buttons for the eyes, one button for the nose
> Embroidery floss for the mouth (we used dark brown)
> Toy stuffing: polyester is fine
> Optional: small scraps of colourful fabric for the triangles

EQUIPMENT

> Sewing machine and thread to match your fabric
> Scissors
> Straight pins
> Rotary cutter, quilter's ruler and self-healing cutting mat
> Measuring tape
> Iron and ironing board
> Unpicker
> Needle
> Optional: air-fading marker
> Knitting needle or chopstick to help turn the monkey out the right way

Let's make it

> Face, tummy, back of head, body: cut four squares 22 cm x 22 cm [8½ inches x 8½ inches]
> Pocket (optional): cut an extra 22 cm x 22 cm [8½ inch x 8½ inch] square from the calico
> Legs: cut four rectangles 60 cm x 10 cm [24 inches x 4 inches]
> Arms: cut two rectangles 60 cm x 10 cm [24 inches x 4 inches]
> Tail: cut one rectangle 60 cm x 10 cm [24 inches x 4 inches]
> Ears: cut two matching pairs from the template in the pocket at the front of the book (four pieces in total)
> Face: cut two eye patches and one nose from the templates in the pocket at the front of the book

1. Make the monkey face

Prepare the shapes for the monkey face. Trace them onto the papery smooth side of your Heat and Bond. Cut the shapes out roughly (not right on the line, yet). Place your chosen fabric wrong side up on the ironing board. Put the roughly cut traced shapes on top of the fabric, with their papery smooth side facing up. Press them onto the fabric with a medium-hot iron. Use firm presses (not back-and-forth motions) so that the shapes don't move. Be sure the edges are well stuck down. Now you need to cut around the shapes, this time right on the line. You'll have a shape with lovely fabric on the front (right side out) and paper on the back. Peel the paper off carefully, then place the fabric right side up on your right-side-up monkey face piece, being sure they are correctly positioned (refer to the photo for placement of features). Press one final time to make them adhere to the face piece. Well done! Now sew around each shape 5 mm [¼ inch] from the raw edge to secure. Now sew your buttons into position firmly, too. Finally stitch a mouth on your monkey, using a bold backstitch. (Draw this on first with a fading maker, if you don't want to stitch freehand.)

2. Triangles for the tummy (optional)

Next make the colourful triangles for the monkey's tummy. Draw the triangles onto the paper side of the Heat and Bond. Then cut around them roughly. Then put them rough side down on the wrong-side-up chosen fabric. Now press as before. Cut them out, neatly this time. Peel the paper off and iron them right side up on the right-side-up monkey tummy.

3. Make the ears

Take two matching ear pieces and, with right sides together, sew a 5 mm [¼ inch] seam around the curved edge only. Sew a second time for strength. You don't need to sew the straight edge. Repeat for the other two matching ear pieces. Clip the curved edges so that they will be neat and curvy when finished. Turn them out the right way and press them well.

4. Sew the monkey tummy to the monkey face

Sew the face piece to the tummy piece, with right sides facing, using a 1 cm [⅜ inch] seam allowance. Sew once more for extra monkey strength. Trim your loose threads. Next, press this seam nice and flat. Stitch a line 5 mm [¼ inch] above and below the seam for a nice neat finish.

5. Attach the ears

Pin and sew the ears to the face as shown. The ears are well away from the top edge (so they don't get caught in the top seam!). Sew with a 5 mm [¼ inch] seam allowance. They should sit nice and flat facing inwards. Don't let them poke outwards (yet!).

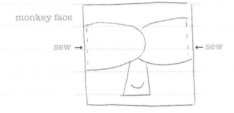

6. Sew the monkey back to the back of the monkey head

Put the square for the back and the square for the back of head together, with their right sides facing. Sew along the bottom raw edge with a 1 cm [⅜ inch] seam. Press the seam flat and trim any loose threads. Now stitch a line 5 mm [¼ inch] above and below the seam for a nice neat finish.

7. Make the pocket for the monkey back (optional)

Take a square of fabric 22 cm x 22 cm [8½ inches x 8½ inches] and with the right side facing up, fold the top edge down 1 cm [⅜ inch]. Press. With the right side still facing you, fold the top edge down again, this time 5 cm [2 inches]. Press. Stitch along the top and bottom folded edges, as shown.

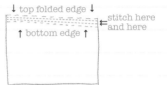

8. Make the tail

Fold your long tail rectangle in half. Stitch down the long side and across the bottom raw edge. Stitch again for extra strength. Turn out and press. Tuck the end of the tail under 1 cm [⅜ inch] to conceal the raw edge. Pin it to the bottom folded edge of the pocket and stitch into place firmly. You need to stitch a rectangle, as illustrated, and then a diagonal line from corner to corner of this stitched square, as shown.

9. Attach the pocket (optional)

Pin the pocket piece, right side up, to the monkey back piece (which is also right side up) with the bottom raw edges aligned. Pin the tail, folded over a couple of times, to the middle of the pocket, well away from the side and bottom seams. Stitch down each side of the pocket (but not along the bottom) to keep it in place for now. Leave the pinned tail in position for now.

10. Make the arms

Fold each long arm rectangle in half widthways, so it forms an even skinnier long rectangle. Sew a 5 mm [¼ inch] seam down the long raw edge. Now sew that same seam again for extra strength. Press the seam flat and sew a little triangle at one end, as shown. Sew those 'triangular' lines once more for strength. Trim. Turn the arm out the right way – this can take a while, so be patient. You can use the wrong end of a knitting needle or a chopstick to help you turn the arm out more easily (and neatly!). Press the arm well and repeat for the other arm.

11. Make the legs

The legs are easier, because we stitch on the outside and we don't need to turn them. Stitch down one long edge, then stitch a curved shape at the bottom of each leg, then back up the other long edge. Repeat again two or three more times. Your stitching doesn't need to be perfect – it's meant to be sketchy and decorative. Now stitch two lines to form the feet, as shown. Trim the corners from the feet to form nice curves close to the stitching.

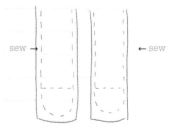

12. Put it all together

Lay your face and body piece right side up. Pin the arms and legs into position (refer to the photo for placement), layering and folding the limbs well away from the edges. The arms should have their seam facing up. Pin everything into place so the pieces don't move near the seams when you sew it all up. The straight raw edge of the arms and legs should match the straight raw edge of the monkey tummy sides and lower edge. Make sure they are evenly spaced too, placing the top edge of the arms level with the seam that joins the tummy and face piece.

Now place the monkey back piece right side down on top, sandwiching the ears, legs, tail and arms inside. It will be a real squish in there, but not to worry, you can do it! Pin well around all four sides and stitch a 1 cm [⅜ inch] seam around only three sides, leaving the top of the head. Stitch around all three sides once more for strength, leaving the top seam open again. Trim your loose threads neatly, remove your pins and turn your monkey right way out. Beware of pins inside – go carefully! Remove any remaining pins and press monkey nicely, avoiding the buttons (they might melt!).

13. Stuff your monkey

Poor monkey. It's okay, he wants to be stuffed, as he's feeling a bit floppy. Take small amounts of stuffing and pop them inside, down into the bottom corners first, and slowly stuff your monkey. Although you might be tempted to stuff him with big bits of stuffing to get quicker results, you'll get a smoother, more evenly stuffed monkey if you use smaller pieces. Make sure you stuff him well, as he will relax a bit once he is sewn up. When you get monkey all full up, fold your top edges inward and begin to hand sew, with lovely small stitches and matching thread, from one corner to the other. As you sew, you can pop in teensy bits of stuffing to make sure he's totally filled up. Keep your stitches small and tight so no stuffing can escape. Sew all the way along the top, taking your time, stitching and stuffing until – voila! He's all done! Well done – go you! Take him to hang out with someone cute you really love.

Note

This monkey is designed for kids aged five and up, as it has long limbs. If you would like to make it for a smaller child, keep it safe: you should embroider the eyes and nose (don't use buttons) and make the limbs much shorter so they can't get tangled around your chosen small child in any way.

▼▼▼▼▼▼▼▼▼▼▼▼▼▼▼▼▼▼▼▼▼▼▼▼▼▼▼▼

Variations

You could make his arms from fuzzier fabric for a cuddlier monkey. You could make some felt bananas to put in his pocket. You could put different shapes on his tummy!

CERAMIC DIY-NAMIC

Porcelain markers are a super-simple way to customise your own crockery. You can keep things really simple and geometric, or you can totally go to town, drawing much fancier things. Once painted and oven baked these ceramics are ready to go. Eat your dinner off them, or hang them on a wall as your very own objet d'art!

MATERIALS

> Porcelain markers: we used Pebeo Porcelaine 150 because they are dishwasher safe and long-lasting. We used the fine point ones
> White crockery: teacups, plates, bowls – whatever you like

EQUIPMENT

> Notepad and pencils
> Window cleaner and a clean, dry cloth
> Water, cotton buds and tissues for cleaning up any errors
> Oven

Let's make it

1. Let's start sketching

First, you need to come up with your design. You can try bold, geometric shapes. Or you can do lovely line drawings. Have a play around with a notepad and pencils until you know what you want to draw. Take your time and come up with something that suits your style.

Next, clean your crockery with window cleaner, making sure it is spotless and super-dry before you begin. Nice work!

2. Now let's draw

Shake each pen well before you use it. Get some scrap paper and give the pen a few good presses to get the ink flowing nicely. Now, draw your design directly on the crockery. Smooth, even pressure is best to avoid any lumps or bumps. If you make a mistake, quickly wipe it off with a damp cotton bud or tissue.

You need to leave your drawn-on crockery to dry for 24 hours. So do that. Tap tap! Tick tock! Is it 24 hours later? Good! Let's finish our project off so that it is dishwasher (mechanical or people-powered!) safe!

3. Heat set your design

Preheat your oven to 150ºC (300ºF). Bake your crockery for 35 minutes. Please do not burn yourself. Remove your crockery and allow it to cool! See how the colours get a bit brighter and shinier after you bake it? Ta-dah! How great are these pens?! Set the table and show off your handiwork!

▼▼▼▼▼▼▼▼▼▼▼▼▼▼▼▼▼▼▼▼▼▼▼▼▼▼▼

Variations

You could decorate ceramic tiles or doodle on some simple knick-knacks if that takes your fancy. Take a step up and learn to use waterslide decals: you can print an image from your computer on your home printer and then apply and seal! How great is that?

ACHILLES THE TORTOISE

In one of my most favourite books, My Family and Other Animals by Gerald Durrell, there is a tortoise called Achilles. He is the nicest tortoise ever, spending his days clambering over teacups and nibbling strawberries and generally being tortoisey. Maybe an Achilles is just what you need in your life? Please avoid wells and other bodies of water if you make this project. (You will need to read the book to find out why.)

MATERIALS

> 3 balls of different-coloured yarn for the shell: we used regular 8 ply [DK] in yellow, pink and green
> 1 ball of yarn for the head and feet: we used regular 8 ply [DK] in black
> 1 bag of toy stuffing
> 1 pair of safety eyes

Finished size: Approximately 30 cm [12 inches] long and 25 cm [10 inches] wide.

EQUIPMENT

> 4 mm [Size 5] crochet hook
> Stitch marker
> Yarn needle
> Scissors

Before you start
If you're new to crochet, see page 138. This book uses Australian and UK crochet terminology, with US terms in square brackets. For a full list of all crochet terms, see page 141. For this project you'll need to know how to do chain, slip stitch, double crochet (DC) and single crochet (SC).

Let's make it

1. Make triangles for the shell

You need to make 12 triangles. Six are for the top of his shell and six are for the bottom. Each group of six will make a hexagon when stitched together!

> Foundation row Chain 3.

> Row one DC [SC] into second chain from hook. DC [SC] into next chain. Chain 1 and turn.

> Row two DC [SC] into first DC [SC]. DC [SC] twice into next DC [SC]. Chain 1 and turn.

> Row three DC [SC] into first DC [SC]. DC [SC] into second DC [SC]. DC [SC] twice into last DC [SC].

> Continue as above. That is, for each row: Chain up 1. DC [SC] once into the first stitch of each row. DC [SC] once into each stitch along the row. And finally DC [SC] twice into the last stitch of each row. You need to make 20 rows like this to complete the triangle.

> Fasten off nice and securely. So, off you go! Make 12 of those triangles – they should all be the same size, please!

2. Sew your triangles together to make the top of Achilles' shell

Arrange your six triangles on your tabletop so that they look nice. Thread your yarn needle with a 30 cm [12 inch] length of yarn. Sew your triangles together two at a time, placing each pair right sides together and stitching their edges with small, neat stitches. When you have three pairs sewn together, stitch each pair to the next to eventually form a hexagon. Repeat with the remaining triangles to form the bottom of the tortoise shell. Bravo!

3. Make the tortoise feet

> Foundation row Chain 11.

> Row one Skip the first stitch and DC [SC] once into each stitch of your foundation row. Chain 1 and turn.

> Continue on, making a total of 10 rows like this (chaining once and then turning at the end of each row).

> Row eleven Decrease once at the beginning of the row: to do this, DC [SC] two stitches together, then DC [SC] once into each stitch, until you reach the last two. Decrease the last two stitches together.

> Row twelve As for row eleven. That's it! Now fasten off your yarn and weave in ends. You need four feet, obviously!

4. Make the tortoise head

> Round one Chain 2. DC [SC] four times into the furthest chain from the hook (it's the first chain stitch that you made!). Slip stitch into the first stitch you made to 'close' the round. Mark this stitch with a stitch marker.

> Round two Chain up 1. DC [SC] twice into each stitch of the previous round. Slip stitch into the stitch you marked to 'close' the round. Move your maker up to your current stitch.

> Round three Chain up 1. *1 DC [SC] into next stitch of previous round, then 2 DC [SC] into the very next stitch over (also in the previous round)*.
> Repeat the pattern between the * and the * until you reach your marker. Slip stitch into the stitch you marked to 'close' the round. Move your maker up to your current stitch.
> Round four Chain up 1. *1 DC [SC] into next stitch, 1 DC [SC] into next stitch, 2 DC [SC] into next stitch*. Repeat the pattern between the * and the * until you reach your marker. Slip stitch into the stitch you marked to 'close' the round.
> Move your maker up to your current stitch.
> Round five Chain up 1. *1 DC [SC] into next stitch, 1 DC [SC] into next stitch, 1 DC [SC] into next stitch, 2 DC [SC] into next stitch*. Repeat the pattern between the * and the * until you reach your marker. Slip stitch into the stitch you marked to 'close' the round. Move your maker up to your current stitch.
> Rounds six to ten DC [SC] once into each stitch, remembering to slip stitch each round closed and move your marker up when you start a new row.
> Slip stitch your final round closed and fasten off securely.
> Attach the eyes through the tortoise head, in their correct positions, making sure they are nice and securely fastened. Stuff the head quite firmly, so that it pleases you and looks like a nice tortoise.

5. Put it all together

> Position the feet on top of the right-side-up tortoise shell bottom as shown in the diagram.

sew like this →

> Stitch the feet into place at each matched edge, with small stitches. Note the feet are all facing inwards.
> Now you need to put a lid on it, by sewing on the top of your tortoise shell. Put your tortoise shell top, right side facing down, atop the just-stitched bottom and feet. All your edges need to be lined up and matching. Make sure all your feet are still tucked in and then stitch around the edges, leaving a gap between the two front legs, for both turning and for inserting the head later. (Note: we have actually stitched the feet twice now, for extra strength!)
> Turn it all the right way out, popping the feet out as you go, and marvel at your headless tortoise.
> Stuff him with small pieces of stuffing until he takes the shape you want. Maybe you like a fat tortoise, or maybe you prefer a trimmer fellow – it's up to you.
> The stuffing will relax a bit over time, so add a bit more than you think you need. Although you might be tempted to stuff him with big bits of stuffing to get quicker results, you'll get a

smoother, more evenly stuffed tortoise if you use smaller pieces. So go slow, like a tortoise!

> Now you need to pop the head into position and use your best mini stitches to sew it securely into place. Use your yarn needle and matching yarn to do this (I used black, yellow and pink yarn). I think?!

> Achilles is quite shy, so I have sewn his head into place so that it only protrudes a little bit. You decide what will work for your tortoise! Now slowly and carefully stitch around the neck and shell a couple of times for extra strength. Excellent! Use your yarn needle to weave in any final yarn ends. Marvel at your amazing tortoise!

Safety note

Even though safety eyes are meant to be safe, if you're making Achilles for children under five years it's a good idea to be extra careful and stitch on felt eyes instead.

Variations

Add a button detail on the top of the shell. Put safety eyes on both sides of the head for a two-sided tortoise (make each side a different colour!). Make a bigger version of Achilles by playing around with sizing the pattern up. Make a scarf for your tortoise if your stitches around the neck are a bit messy. Make a massive Achilles from 20 ply [super-bulky] yarn, or the thickest yarn you can find, for a rather fantastic footstool or child's seat!

HUCKLEBERRY BOTTLE TOTES

I think that those brown bags they give you when you buy a nice bottle of wine do not cut the mustard. These fabric bottle totes are much nicer. You can even tie them together and secure them firmly to the handlebars of your bike (ride carefully!). Not just for wine, these are also very happy with a bottle of icy ginger beer or lemonade stowed inside.

FABRIC DETAILS

Finished size: To fit a standard 750 ml [24 fl oz] bottle: approximately 16 cm x 33 cm [6¼ inches x 13 inches].

Seam allowance: Seam allowance is 1 cm [⅜ inch] unless otherwise stated.

Before you sew: Fabric should be washed, dried and pressed nicely before cutting and sewing. This will prevent fabric shrinkage and dyes running.

MATERIALS

> One fat quarter of cotton fabric (a fat quarter measures about 50 cm x 56 cm [18 x 22 inches]). Or use a couple of fat quarters if you want to mix things up (like in our photo) or make two at a time!

EQUIPMENT

> Sewing machine and thread to match your fabric
> Scissors
> Straight pins
> Measuring tape
> Iron and ironing board

Cutting it out

Fold and cut the fat quarter as shown in our diagram, to make the bag pieces.

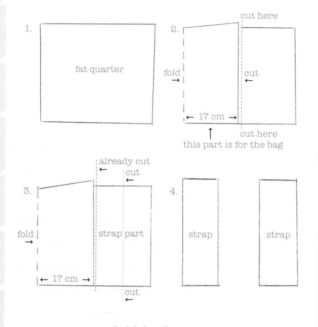

1. Make the strap

Place your two strap pieces together with all raw edges matching and right sides facing. Pin and stitch a 1 cm [⅜ inch] seam at one short end. Remove pin, snip loose threads and press this seam open. Now fold the strap in half lengthways and press in a firm crease. Unfold the fabric again and marvel at the lovely crease you pressed down the middle of the strap. Well done you!

Now you need to fold each long raw edge in to meet this crease. Fold one side in first and press,

then fold the other side in, again pressing where you folded. Hurrah! It will look like this picture.

Fold your strap in half lengthways once more and pin it together securely along the full length of the strap. Top-stitch the strap 2–3 mm [about ⅛ inch] from where the two folded edges meet, all the way along the length of the strap once more. Now top-stitch 2–3 mm [about ⅛ inch] in along the other long edge to make it look nice and neat. Trim the raw ends neatly and tie them in a knot.

2. Position and attach the strap

Trim your bag piece so that it measures 34 cm x 40 cm [13½ inches x 16 inches]. (You can keep the extra bit and make it into a pocket if you like!) Press your bag piece in half widthways to create a nice pressed-in centre crease. Unfold. Bring the folded edge into the centre crease and press again, creating a quarter crease! Measure 25 cm [10 inches] up from the bottom edge of your bag piece and pin the centre of your strap to the pressed-in quarter crease of your bag piece (at the 25 cm [10 inch] mark). Make sure the best side of the strap is facing upwards. Stitch into place securely, making a little rectangle and then stitching diagonal lines as in the diagram.

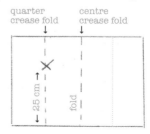

3. Sew up the bag

With the right side facing away from you, fold the top edge down 2 cm [¾ inch] and press. Fold down another 2 cm [¾ inch] and press. Pin and top-stitch into place 2–3 mm [about ⅛ inch] from the bottom folded edge. Next, pin the straps to the just-stitched edge so that they are away from the side and bottom seams. With right sides facing up, fold your bag piece in half widthways. Pin and stitch a sturdy 2.5 cm [1 inch] seam along the bottom of the bag. Stitch once more for extra strength. Now stitch a 1 cm [⅜ inch] seam up the side, matching your raw edges neatly and making sure your straps are well away from where you are stitching. Stitch the side seam once more and trim your loose threads. Turn your bag the right way out, remove any stray pins and press. Now pop in a bottle of pop (or a bottle of wine if you are old enough!).

Variations

Make two of these from different fabrics and switch the straps so that your fabric contrasts. Add a pocket. Try varying spots and stripes ... or checks and florals! Use this basic idea to make these bags from any lovely fabric, vintage sheeting, old tablecloths, even favourite worn-out dresses!

GEOGRAPHY SEAT

You really do not have to have the same stool as everybody else. You can customise your perch to suit you. I think this map stool is a much nicer way of finding your way around than a gps. And it's much more useful when you have tired feet. I made this one with a map of the north west of Western Australia (where I used to live). Maybe you could chart your own life with these cute stools too? You could use this idea to cover a bedhead or a little table too, couldn't you?

MATERIALS

> Vintage or new wooden stool
> Vintage or new map
> Mod Podge or PVA glue: do not shake your glue or Mod Podge! Air bubbles may form
> Découpage sealer (or more Mod Podge!)

EQUIPMENT

> Foam brush
> Newspaper or butcher's paper for template
> Scissors
> Blu-Tack
> A pin

1. Prepare your template

Measure the seat of your stool. We need to make a template from the newspaper, so draw the shape of your seat up exactly and cut it out. Put your newspaper template atop your stool and make sure it's a good fit. If it isn't, back to the drawing board and try again.

2. Cut out your map shape

Take your template and place it on top of your map. You want to make sure that you are using your very favourite part of the map. Blu-Tack the template into position on the map and cut around the template carefully with sharp scissors and a steady hand.

3. Glue your map to your stool

Apply your Mod Podge or PVA glue sparingly to the stool, starting at the top edge and applying it slowly all the way down your stool. Make sure it's nicely smoothed out and lump free. Put your map atop the glue and carefully smooth out any air bubbles, continue working your way downwards, applying slowly and carefully and then smoothing your map down. If any air bubbles do form, smooth them out with your fingers. Allow your stool to dry for at least 2 hours. (Use a pin to prick the centre of any stubborn remaining air bubbles.)

4. Seal your stool

Apply three or four more coats of Mod Podge or découpage sealer to your stool, allowing each coat to dry thoroughly before starting on the next.

Variations

You could do this to a little side table ... or even a big table! Try something other than a map for the stool top, maybe vintage storybook pages, old newspapers or lovely wallpaper. Make a whole set of these for the cutest dinner party seating!

GEOGRAPHY SEAT

TINY SAILBOAT NAPKINS

I think that napkins totally fancy up a table. Hand-embroidered napkins even more so. Stitch these in front of the telly and you'll have a fancy table in no time at all. These boats would be perfect stitched onto a super cosy towel for a new baby, too. Make sure you hand wash these in cold water to keep them looking nice.

MATERIALS

> Two plain fabric napkins: linen or cotton is best (or see my notes at the end of this project on how to make your own)
> Stranded embroidery floss in a few nice colours

EQUIPMENT

> Air-fading fabric marker
> Needle
> Scissors
> Iron and ironing board

Let's make it

1. Prepare your napkin

First, press your napkin so that it's nice and neat and flat. Let it cool down and put it right side up on your work surface. Using the boats on this page as a guide, draw your triangles onto the napkin with an air-fading fabric marker. It's best to draw them just in one corner, so that when you fold the napkin you will be able to see all of your design.

2. Embroider

Take your chosen embroidery floss and cut a length of about 30 cm [12 inches]. Next, separate the strands of floss until you have only two. Thread these two strands through your needle and begin stitching your triangles with satin stitch. You need to stitch long stitches very close together, being sure you pay attention to your outline. The stitches will shimmy up next to each other and slowly 'colour in' your triangle. Take your time and you'll get a nice, neat, blocked-in result.

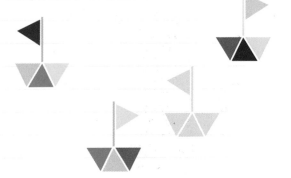

3. Finish your embroidery nicely

When you have finished stitching, bring your needle through to the wrong side of your napkin. Carefully weave the needle in and out of the underside of your embroidery, between the stitches you made. Weave one way, pulling your floss through neatly (but not too tightly!). Now weave the other way. Snip your loose end very close to your work to finish.

4. Stitch more triangles

Continue on like this, stitching your triangles in different colours and different sizes. Be sure to finish your work neatly by weaving in your ends and snipping the excess floss. Behold your lovely napkins! Don't they make you want to have people over for dinner? I think you should do that!

Variations

You can vary the embroidery in any way you like! You could appliqué cute shapes if you are a bit too tired to embroider. Or you could use fabric markers to fancy your napkins up ... or tapestry yarn and a big needle ... or even machine stitch random lines across your napkins!

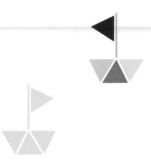

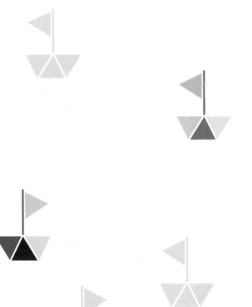

Materials and equipment

> A square of linen or cotton 2 cm [1 inch] larger than your desired finished napkin size
> Sewing machine and thread to match your fabric
> Scissors
> Straight pins
> Iron and ironing board
> Needle

Let's make it

1. Let's work one side at a time. Fold your first side in 1 cm [⅜ inch] and press. Now fold this pressed-in edge over 1 cm [⅜ inch] a second time. Press well and pin to secure. Neatly stitch this edge down 5 mm [¼ inch] from the folded edge. Repeat for each side, being careful to tuck the excess fabric in at the corners before you stitch over it. You can also stop just before the corner, then tuck your excess fabric in and hand stitch it for a super-neat finish.

2. Press your napkin and then think about ways to make it look cute!

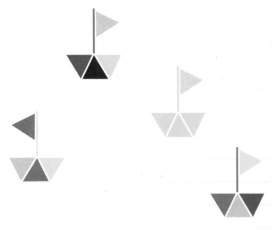

CHEERY CHESSBOARD

Not to be confused with a Cheery Cheese Board, which is also a good thing, but perhaps a project for a different kind of book. Whether it is chess or cheese that you are into, I guarantee that my Chessboard is the happiest, most useful you will ever see. You can make it any colour you like! I think pink would be quite amazing, but not for cheese, just for chess.

FABRIC DETAILS

Finished size: Approximately 48 cm x 50 cm [19 inches x 20 inches].

Seam allowance: Seam allowance is 1 cm [⅜ inch] unless otherwise stated.

Before you sew: Fabric should be washed, dried and pressed nicely before cutting and sewing. This will prevent fabric shrinkage and dyes running.

MATERIALS

> 50 cm x 55 cm [20 inches x 22 inches] of unbleached calico for bag front
> 50 cm x 55 cm [20 inches x 22 inches] fabric for bag back
> Permaset fabric ink in your chosen colour (yellow, pink, magenta?!)
> Chess pieces: try the dollar store or eBay
> About 1.5 m [1½ yards] cord for drawstring
> Two identical foam squares measuring 5 cm x 5 cm [2 inches x 2 inches] for printing and 'spacing': or you can use a cut-up kitchen sponge

EQUIPMENT

> Old newspaper
> Air-fading fabric marker or tailor's chalk
> Measuring tape
> Disposable silicone gloves to protect your hands from the ink
> An old plastic container to pour the ink into
> Paintbrush
> Iron and ironing board
> Sewing machine and thread to match your fabric
> Scissors
> Straight pins
> Rotary cutter, quilter's ruler and self-healing cutting mat
> Large safety pin

Let's make it

Lay your calico piece on a clean work surface and put some layers of newspaper underneath it to prevent the ink from seeping through. Mark a nice even square in the centre of your fabric with your fading marker or tailor's chalk. It needs to measure 40 cm x 40 cm [16 inches x 16 inches]. Make sure it's a perfect square for best results – if it's a bit crooked, your chessboard will be crooked (although that's not the end of the world, is it?).

1. Let's start printing

Put your gloves on! Pour some of your ink into the container and dip the sponge into it. Starting in the top left corner of your marked-out square, and using the template in the pocket at the front of the book as a guide, we will begin stamping our squares on! Line the sponge up with the corner and press down firmly to print. Use your paintbrush to dab on extra ink over any patchy areas. Place your other square of sponge neatly directly under the square you just stamped, as a spacer, marking the area you don't want to print. Make sure you are lined up with the original line you marked on the left-hand side and be sure that your square is straight. Now repaint your inky square and line it up underneath the 'spacer' square. Print again. Then space, then print, following the template. Don't be upset if things don't line up perfectly. It will still be perfectly fabulous for playing chess on. Just try

to keep things as straight as you can. Once you have printed all the rows of your chessboard, let it dry overnight. Next, use a medium-hot iron to carefully press your printed squares and set the ink. Be careful not to singe your fabric, though!

2. Now we need to make it into a bag

Firstly, place your chessboard fabric piece right side up and your back fabric panel on top of it, right side down. Got that? They should be on top of each other with right sides facing, short sides at the top and bottom and all sides matching. Perfect. Pin around three sides with lots of pins, leaving the top edge open. Stitch a 1 cm [⅜ inch] seam around the pinned three sides. Remove the pins and stitch the same three seams once more for extra durability. Snip your loose threads and give it all a nice press with a medium-hot iron. Good work, petals!

3. Let's make the casing for the drawstring

With right sides still facing in, tuck the top raw edge down 5 mm [¼ inch] and press well. Pin into place and stitch carefully all the way around to make a nice neat edge. Remove your pins and trim your loose threads. Now fold your top edge down once more, this time a full 2.5 cm [1 inch]. This creates the casing to thread your drawstring through. Pin the edge again, just like we did before, but note that we are not going to stitch all the way around this time! We are going to stitch nearly all the way around, as neatly as we can and very close to the bottom folded and stitched edge. When you begin stitching, make sure to stitch back and forth a couple of times to keep the casing secure. Once you have stitched almost all the way around, and are a full 2.5 cm [1 inch] away from where you started, STOP! Remember to leave a gap where you can insert your drawstring and thread it through the length of the casing. Stitch back and forth where you stopped stitching to finish the seam (leaving a gap), snip your threads and then whisk your bag away from the machine. Trim all your loose inside-bag threads and turn it all out the right way. Press well.

4. Now we'll thread the drawstring

Pin a safety pin to one end of the cord. Push the safety pin into the gap you left. Keep pushing it gently through the casing, easing the fabric if it's a bit stubborn and bunched up, and thread it all the way through and back out the gap you left. Gently pull the cord right through the casing and adjust your fabric so that it is all cute and evenly gathered. Tie the ends of the cord together and trim the ends.

5. That's it!

Plonk your chess pieces inside and give it a good shake – because that makes a nice noise. Now find someone to play with! Yippee!

Variations

Maybe you could appliqué your squares, instead of printing them? You could use printed fabrics or plain, as long as the squares are all arranged correctly. You could use fabric markers to colour your squares in, rather than printing them. You could use this board for checkers (draughts) as well, as both checkers and chess have 8 x 8 squares!

NANNA BAUBLES

I first made these when Frankie magazine asked me to decorate a Christmas tree for their festive issue. How cosy do these look? Don't get me wrong, regular baubles are really quite lovely, but it's always good to have a 'cardigan', isn't it?

MATERIALS

> 6 cm [2½ inch] Christmas baubles with wire hangers
> A few balls of yarn in pretty colours: fine baby yarn works well, or regular 8 ply [DK] is good too
> 2 m [2 yards] of ribbon (which will hang ten baubles)

EQUIPMENT

> 3.5 mm [Size 4] crochet hook
> Wool needle
> Scissors

Before you start
If you're new to crochet, see page 138. This book uses Australian and UK crochet terminology, with US terms in square brackets. For a full list of all crochet terms, see page 141. For this project you'll need to know how to do chain, slip stitch, double crochet (DC) and single crochet (SC).

1. Foundation ring

This is the ring that begins it all! Make a slip knot and put it on your hook. Pull it firmly (but not tightly). Chain 5 and then slip stitch into the very first chain you made to form a ring. Bravo!

2. Round one

Chain up 3 stitches to begin the next round. Now treble [double crochet] 15 times into the ring you made. You will now have 15 treble [double crochet] and the original 3 chain stitches you made. And you will have 1 loop on your hook. To close the round, make a slip stitch into the third chain you made (when you chained up) and fasten off.

3. Round two

Chain up 3 stitches once more to begin round two. Now treble [double crochet] 2 stitches into the very first of the chain stitches you just made. You have made a cluster! We're going to crochet into the stitches of the round below now. Skip the stitch next to the cluster you just made (working anti-clockwise around the round). Treble [double crochet] 3 times into the next stitch (the stitch after the one you just skipped). You now have a cluster and a gap and a cluster! Continue around the circle with this pattern: skip 1, treble [double crochet] 3 times into the next stitch, skip 1, treble [double crochet] 3 times into the

next stitch. When you have 8 clusters you are done. Slip stitch the round closed as before, by hooking into the top chain stitch (where you chained up for this round) and pulling a loop of that stitch through the loop that is already on your hook.

4. Round three

For this round we are going to make 8 clusters again: this time by hooking into the 'gaps' in the previous round. And we are going to have two chain stitches between our clusters, to allow for the round middle of our bauble. So here we go ... Chain up 3 stitches. Treble [double crochet] 2 into the closest 'gap' between a pair of clusters (in the round below!). Then chain 2 stitches. Treble [double crochet] 3 into the next 'gap'. Chain 2 stitches. Treble [double crochet] 3 into the next 'gap' once more. Continue around the circle until you have 8 clusters again. Chain 2 and slip stitch as before to close the round.

5. Round four

Chain up 3 stitches. Then repeat the exact same pattern as for Round 3. Chain 2. Treble [double crochet] 3 into the 'gap' below. Chain 2. Treble [double crochet] 3 into the 'gap' below. Do this all the way around until you have 8 clusters and gaps. Slip stitch closed as before.

6. Round five

Now you are going to start decreasing to shape the top of the bauble cosy, which is why we're reverting to just 1 chain in each gap. Chain up 3 to start a new round. Treble [double crochet] 2 into the nearest gap. Chain 1. Treble [double crochet] 3 into the gap below. Chain 1. Treble [double crochet] 3 into the next gap below. Continue in this pattern until you have 8 clusters once more. Slip stitch the round closed as before.

7. Round six

This is the same as round five! So do that again – off you go!

8. Grab your tail

Now STOP! Have a look at what you did! You have made a cup-shaped bauble cosy, ready to have a bauble tucked inside! Before you do that, pull your loose yarn tail (from where you started your crochet) through to the outside of your work. You can just poke your hook in and pull it through.

9. Tuck your bauble in

Pull your yarn loop nice and long so you don't lose it! You need it later to finish crocheting the bauble safely inside. Carefully put your bauble into the crocheted form, with the hanger at the top. Don't let your work unravel or lose the loop that you are going to crochet with again in a minute.

10. Crochet your bauble closed

Put your hook back through your loosened loop and pull the yarn so that the loop is nice and firm once more and ready to crochet on with. Now you need to double crochet [single crochet] once into each 'gap' in the round below to secure your crochet and keep your bauble snug in its jacket. Pull your yarn nice and tight after each stitch to ensure a cosy fit. When you have worked all the way around, slip stitch into the nearest gap and snip your yarn off, leaving a tail of 20 cm [8 inches] or so.

11. Hide your yarn tails

Grab your wool needle and thread the top loose yarn tail through its nice plump eye. Carefully use the needle to weave the yarn tail in among the nearest cluster, first one way, then another for extra security. Pull the tail tight and snip it close to the work so that the tail disappears. Do the same thing with the tail at the bottom of the bauble. Thread a loop of ribbon through the hanger and tie the ribbon in a firm knot about 10 cm [4 inches] from where you threaded it through.

Variations

You could use this concept to crochet a cosy for a pet rock, an apple, an orange ... for lots of things really! You could also make these with finer yarn for a lovely delicate doily kind of look.

CRAFTY HOW-TOS

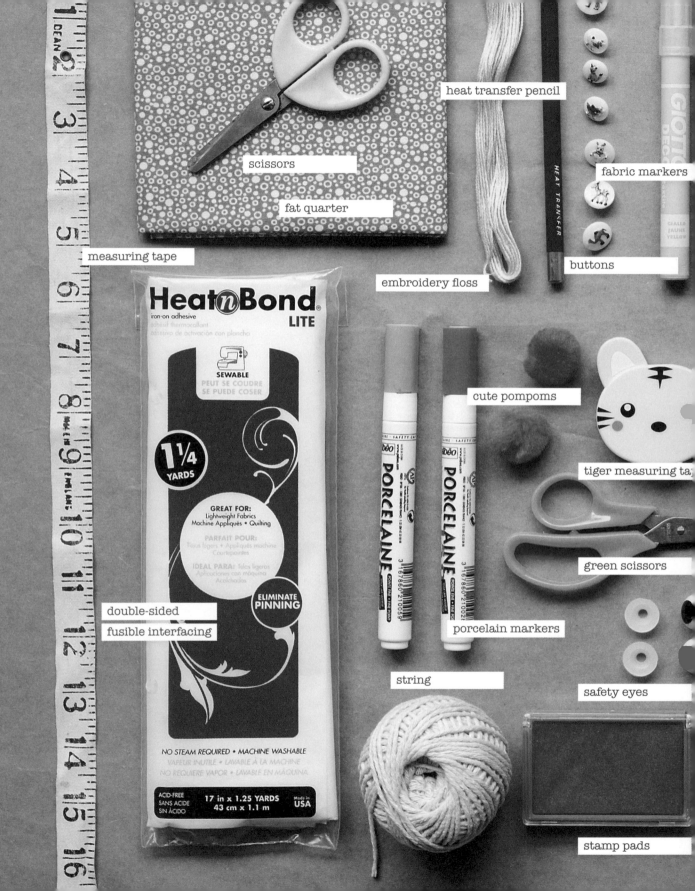

measuring tape

scissors

fat quarter

heat transfer pencil

fabric markers

buttons

embroidery floss

HeatnBond LITE
iron-on adhesive
adhésif thermocollant
adhesivo de activación con plancha

SEWABLE
PEUT SE COUDRE
SE PUEDE COSER

1¼ YARDS

GREAT FOR:
Lightweight Fabrics
Machine Appliqués • Quilting

PARFAIT POUR:
Tissus légers • Appliqués machine
Courtepointes

IDEAL PARA: Telas ligeras
Aplicaciones con máquina
Acolchados

ELIMINATE PINNING

NO STEAM REQUIRED • MACHINE WASHABLE
VAPEUR INUTILE • LAVABLE À LA MACHINE
NO REQUIERE VAPOR • LAVABLE EN MÁQUINA

ACID-FREE
SANS ACIDE
SIN ÁCIDO

17 in x 1.25 YARDS
43 cm x 1.1 m

Made in USA

double-sided

fusible interfacing

cute pompoms

tiger measuring tape

PORCELAINE

PORCELAINE

green scissors

porcelain markers

string

safety eyes

stamp pads

hama bead boards

mod podge

crochet hooks

yarn needle

fabric markers

knitting needles

button

measuring tape

e-z cut carving medium fox

ribbon

lino cutting tools

button

scalpel/craft knife

cute pom poms

washi tape

ir-fading fabric markers

fabric ink

stamp pad

quilting pins

origami paper

Stitch library

It's good to have a repertoire of stitches to play around with when you are being crafty. This will help you to be a really good stitch show off, like me. Be sure to check out YouTube for a ton of video tutorials on all these basic stitches. I find watching someone stitch makes a lot more sense than diagrams. Maybe you will find that too!

Whip stitch

A simple over-and-over stitch that can be used to make a hem or close an opening. Keep stitches small and even for best results and knot off securely at the end, making small extra-tight stitches for security.

Useful basic stitches

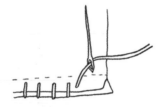

Overcast stitch

Overcast stitch involves stitching over the edges of the fabric to neaten a raw edge and prevent fraying. You need to make a nice, even, over-and-over stitch through both edges of your fabric. Keep your stitches nice and small for best results.

Top-stitch

Top-stitching involves finishing a sewn piece by stitching a line of regular old straight stitches (at the required seam allowance). It provides a nice finish and can be done by hand or by machine.

Pretty embroidery stitches

Backstitch

Backstitch is a really neat, easy stitch. It's a simple way to outline your design with a solid line. If you don't have a sewing machine, backstitch is also a good sturdy stitch for seams. You need to keep your stitches the same length for best results. To backstitch, stitch one stitch, then bring the needle up through the fabric a stitch length away from the previous stitch. Take your needle back down into the end of the previous stitch. Now off you go again – up a stitch length away from the previous stitch, and back down into the end of the previous stitch. You're doing the backstitch!

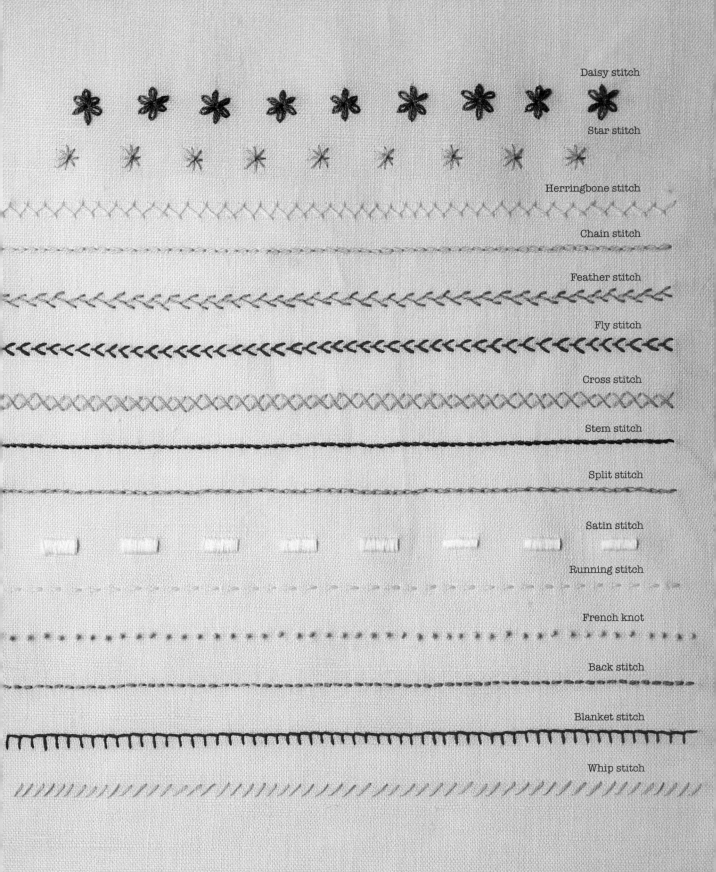

Daisy stitch

Star stitch

Herringbone stitch

Chain stitch

Feather stitch

Fly stitch

Cross stitch

Stem stitch

Split stitch

Satin stitch

Running stitch

French knot

Back stitch

Blanket stitch

Whip stitch

Blanket stitch

Blanket stitch is fantastic for finishing edges and stitching around curves in a decorative way. Bring your needle up through the fabric, then push it though the top of your work about 5 mm [¼ inch] diagonally opposite your entry point, then back up another 5 mm [¼ inch] from this point, level with your original entry point. Pull your floss through, looping the thread under the needle to form a blanket stitch.

French knot

A seemingly tricky stitch, but it's simple when you know how! Bring your threaded and knotted needle up through to the top of your work. Pull the floss right through the fabric firmly. Lay your needle across the spot next to where your thread just came through the fabric. Now wind the floss around the needle three or four times at the pointy end, keeping your thread tight and your needle in place. This wound-around floss will form most of your French

knot. Next, carefully pull the wound-around thread down to the eye end of the needle – away from the pointy end. Keep pulling it down and over the eye, being sure it's pulled tight and all bunched together as it comes off the end of the needle and is nearly level with the fabric. Now stitch into the fabric again very close to where you originally came up to form the 'knot'! Bravo!

Running stitch

A lovely naïve under-and-over stitch you may have learnt in kindergarten! If not, here's how. Make a stitch by pushing the needle up from under your work, then back down a nice stitch length away, then leave a stitch-length gap and come up again with your needle, and then back down – continuing on with an even, gappy stitch.

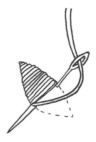

Satin stitch

A great stitch for filling in areas that need 'colouring in'. Satin stitch consists of long, straight, fine stitches within an outline. Keep your stitches very close beside each other.

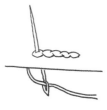

Split stitch is the Splitsville sister of backstitch. It looks like a little chain and is another good stitch for outlining designs. To make a split stitch, knot your floss and make one short first stitch, up through your work and then down into the fabric. Now, push your needle back up through the centre of this first short stitch, thus splitting the stitch. Next, push your needle back down into your work an even stitch length away from the last stitch – now 'split' back up through the middle of the previous stitch – thus each new stitch splits the last.

Stem stitch

Working from left to right, bring your needle up through the fabric. Then poke the needle into the fabric a stitch length away to mark the end of the stitch. The needle then spikes back through the fabric (still working on the top side of your fabric, but from right to left) halfway between where you came up and where you inserted the needle to end the stitch. Pull through and make your next stitch ending, then spike through halfway again to make a

second stitch. Continue on like this, being sure that each stitch starts at previous stitch.

Cross stitch

Make a diagonal stitch from lower left to upper right. Then make a diagonal stitch from lower right to upper left. Make sure the stitches are the same length, so that their tops and bottoms are level. Now you have a lovely cross! If you are making a row of stitches, first make all the diagonals from left to right. Then retrace your stitches finishing the crosses with a diagonal right to left stitch.

Fly stitch

Bring the needle up through the fabric at the top left corner of your stitch-to-be. Push the needle back into the fabric at the top right corner of your stitch-to-be. The needle tip should point downwards, towards the bottom of the stitch. Pull the needle through over the thread to form a V shape. Work a tiny straight stitch to hold the loop in place and secure the V shape.

Feather stitch

Imagine or actually draw (use your air-fading fabric marker!) four lines to indicate where your stitches should begin and end. Make your first V shaped stitch, using the base of the stitch to form the next stitch (which is over to the left). The base of this stitch will then form part of the next stitch (which is over to the right!). The tops of your V need to be level for each stitch. The previous stitch always begins the next stitch.

Chain stitch

Bring your needle and thread up through the fabric. Hold your thread against the fabric with your thumb, making a neat (but unsecured) loop shape. Now insert the needle back into the exact same point where it last emerged and then bring the point back out again, a stitch length away. Pull the thread through, keeping the working thread under the needle point to form a chain shape.

Herringbone stitch

Bring your needle up through your fabric at 1, then down again at 2 and up once more at 3. Push the needle down at 4 and up through the fabric once more at 5. Basically you are making diagonal lines secured by loops underneath the fabric. The tops and bottoms of each stitch should be level.

Star stitch

The pretty star stitch is made up of eight straight stitches of the same length, all worked in to the same central point.

Daisy stitch

Form a series of chain stitches around a central point or central circle (see chain stitch).

Sewing basics

There is so much to learn about sewing. Here are some of the basics we cover in this book. Don't let new terms and techniques befuddle you. Make a cup of tea, put on your thinking cap and think of this as a crafty adventure. Let's go!

Air-fading fabric marker

One of my favourite things ever, an air-fading fabric marker is a cool, magical pen that fades away after a day or two. It's perfect for marking fabric for embroidery. Buy them from your favourite sewing store or online. Always buy a reputable brand as sometimes the cheaper ones don't fade out!

Appliqué

Appliqué is all about attaching one piece of pretty fabric to another piece of fabric, and appliquer means 'to put on' in French. There are many ways to appliqué. You can simply hand stitch. You can use fusible interfacing and a hot iron to adhere your fabrics to each other. Or you can machine sew. Appliqué is a cute way to customise your projects.

This is how to appliqué. You'll need some double-sided iron-on fusible interfacing: try Vliesofix or Therm O Web Heat and Bond or Heat and Bond Lite. Have a chat to your friendly sewing store staff to be sure you choose the right kind, as some are easier to use than others. (Some are super-thick and hard to stitch through, while others are easy peasy!) Draw or trace your design onto the papery side of the interfacing. Cut around this shape 1 cm [⅜ inch] from the traced or drawn outline. Now place the shape, shiny side down, onto the wrong side of your chosen fabric. Press with a hot iron so that the interfacing adheres to the wrong side of the fabric. Cut out your shape, right along the traced or drawn line. Now peel the backing paper from the wrong side of the cut-out shape, revealing the adhesive underneath. Place your shape, sticky side down, onto the right side of your sewing project, in the exact spot you want to appliqué it to. The right side of your shape is facing up. Press it again with the iron. Finish by hand stitching decoratively around the edge; or, if you don't need a decorative finish, machine stitch just inside the edge. You can layer details of the design by following the same procedure, adding windows to a house shape you've applied first, or a door, or whatever you like!

Baste

Mmm, delicious, but no. This is a different kind of baste. When you use basting stitches (also known as tacking stitches), you are sewing nice, long running stitches to temporarily hold your fabric pieces together. Later you will stitch permanently then remove the basting stitches with a seam ripper. I like to baste things when I'm feeling a bit hesitant, in case I'm sewing something incorrectly. Then I go back and stitch over with proper stitches when I'm sure I've got it right. Think of basting as a trial run for the hesitant sewer!

Bias Binding

Welcome to the super-tidy world of bias binding (also known as bias tape). Bias binding is a thin strip of fabric that folds over the raw edges of your garment or project to finish them nicely. It's called bias binding because it's cut on the bias (which means at a 45-degree angle to the selvedge). This means it's stretchier and more flexible than fabric which is cut straight. You can buy bias binding pre-made or make your own using a bias tape maker. It comes in a packet or off the roll in the length and width you choose.

Buttons

You will be everyone's friend if you can reattach a button with aplomb. So let's do that! To sew on a button, thread your needle with 30 cm [12 inches] or so of matching thread and knot the end. Check the position of the button carefully (you can mark it with a pin or tailor's chalk if you like). Sew a couple of neat stitches on the right side of the fabric to 'anchor' your button. Now thread the button the right way up onto the needle so that it shimmies down into position. Sew carefully five or six times through each pair of holes. Some buttons have only one pair of holes, while others have two. Then take your thread through to the back of your work and sew four or five tiny stitches to make your button super-sturdy and secure. Tie off your thread with a firm knot and trim.

Embroidery

Stitcharama! Embroidery, as you probably know, covers the whole gamut of decorative stitching on fabric projects. It can be simple running stitch à la kindergarten, or it can be more complex and refined. We recommend taking a look at www.sublimestitching.com for all sorts of tricks, tips and embroidery how-tos! See our Stitch Library on pages 118–22. See also Transferring an embroidery design onto fabric.

Embroidery floss

The silky spectrum of embroidery floss, or thread, comes in many different types. Where the projects in this book specify embroidery floss, we recommend stranded cotton, a six-stranded thread for embroidery projects. It comes in lots of colours and the thread can be used as is, or split into a few strands (or even a single strand) to create heavy or fine stitches. You can also combine strands of two or more colours to get fancy effects. I like fancy things, perhaps you do too?

Embroidery hoop

A hoopy friend to hold your stitching taut. An embroidery hoop consists of a pair of hoops made from metal, wood, bamboo or plastic. The two hoops fasten together, sandwiching your embroidery fabric

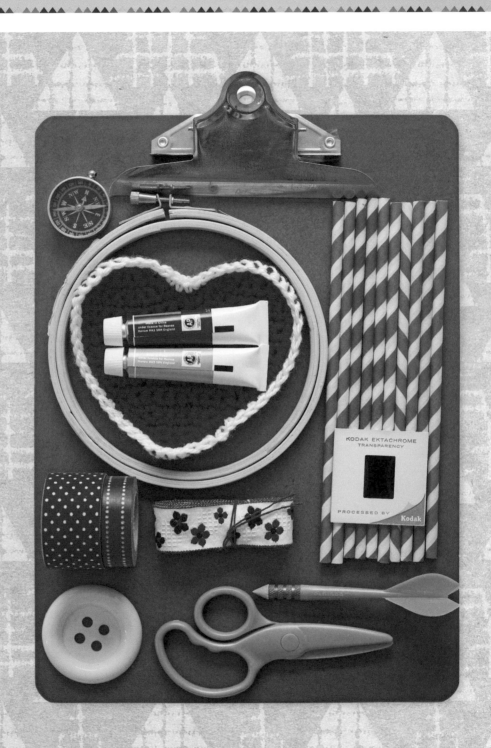

in between. When your fabric is stretched tightly it helps you to make neat, even stitches. A smallish hoop around 15–20 cm [6–8 inches] is best.

How to use an embroidery hoop

Unscrew the two pieces of the hoop and place the inner hoop on a clean, flat surface. Drape your fabric right side up over it, making sure the design is centred in the hoop. Now squish the still-unscrewed outer hoop down over the top, loosely sandwiching the fabric between the two hoop pieces. The screw should be at the top and centre to stop your thread from catching as you stitch. Don't force it as the hoop could snap! Tighten the screw, pulling the fabric as you do until it's taut. Now embroider away! Once you've embroidered all the area within the hoop, unscrew the hoop and reposition it over another part of the fabric. The hoop might flatten part of your embroidery. Don't worry; you'll be able to steam it back to life later. Place a clean white towel or piece of calico on your ironing board. Place your finished piece of embroidery face down on top of it, fold up the other end of the towel to cover it, then press.

Fabric

You can buy new fabric or you can reuse fabric from items you already have. You could also buy vintage fabric from second hand stores or online. We recommend 100 per cent natural fibres such as cotton, but ask at your fabric store if you aren't sure. All fabric should be washed, dried and pressed before using to prevent dyes from running and to allow for fabric shrinkage. All hand-sewn items should be hand washed in warm (not hot!) water to prolong their life.

Fat quarter

If you take a metre [yard] of fabric and cut it in halves both horizontally and vertically, you end up with four 'fat quarters'. Fat quarters are available pre-cut from fabric stores, especially patchwork stores. Be careful, because fat quarters are often cut in wildly differing sizes and with crazy crooked edges, despite all starting from that first metre [yard]. Measure and trim them to suit your project.

Pinking shears

These are saw-toothed scissors that make a lovely zigzag cut. They are used for finishing edges and help to prevent fabric from fraying.

Pressing

You must press as you go – you must! If you don't have an iron, knock on the neighbour's door and borrow one. Pressing your work as you go is vital. It helps keep your seams neat and nice, and it makes your sewing project look way more professional. Apparently it also 'sets' your seams. Imagine that. Get set, I say!

Press studs

Press studs are a simple way to 'close' a garment or a project. They are a less fussy than buttons and button holes and good for beginner sewers. To sew on a press stud, thread your needle with about 30 cm [12 inches] of thread to match your fabric. Check the position of the press stud pieces carefully. Mark the positions with tailor's chalk on the upper and lower parts of your sewing project. Sew the pointing-out (male!) part of the press-stud to the upper part of your work, making four or five tiny, firm stitches through each hole. Tie off the thread tightly and trim the loose end. Double check the position of the other press-stud piece (and make sure it's the right way out, so that the two pieces snap together), then repeat the sewing process. Tie off firmly and trim.

Quilting

To stitch through all the layers of your quilt by hand or with a sewing machine. A quilter's ruler is often used. It is a transparent plastic ruler with inches marked at even increments along its length. It's an invaluable tool for cutting straight lines, and is used with a rotary cutter and a self-healing cutting mat.

Raw edge

The unfinished, freshly cut or torn edge of fabric.

Reverse stitch

To stitch backwards with your sewing machine for extra-secure stitches. Do this at the ends of each seam for strength and to prevent your stitches from unravelling. If you're hand sewing a seam, make a few backstitches at the start and end of the seam.

Rotary cutter

A really super-useful tool, well worth the investment! A rotary cutter is a circular, rotating cutting blade with a handle. Rotary cutters are used with a metal or quilting ruler and a self-healing cutting mat for best results. They're great – indeed, they are happiest! – when they're cutting several layers of fabric. This method is quick and accurate; however, as a rotary cutter is essentially a circular razor blade, take care when using it. Always replace the safety guard after every cut.

Scissors

Keep one pair for cutting fabric, one pair for paper, one pair for random craft and a tiny pair for embroidery and other fiddly bits. A pair of pinking shears is useful for neatening cut edges of fabric.

Seam

The line created by joining two pieces of fabric together. The seam is where the two pieces of fabric meet, and is created by the stitches. Seams are often pressed flat on the inside to keep them neat.

Seam ripper

Also known as a stitch ripper, stitch unpicker or 'quick unpick', this is a marvellous little tool for unpicking wayward, wonky or mistaken stitches. Think of them as your rewind button – they'll take you back to the bit you were happy with and will undo your stitchy errors.

Self-healing cutting mat

A ruled and marked plastic cutting surface that absorbs any nicks or cuts made by sharp blades. It's good to have a small one and a nice big one if you plan on doing lots of sewing. They are especially useful for patchwork.

Selvedge

The woven, neatly finished straight edge of your fabric. The selvedge is sometimes printed with the fabric maker, design and other information. Selvedges shrink at a greater rate than the rest of the fabric when washed, so it's a good idea to cut them off rather than incorporate them into your project.

Sewing machine

Get to know your machine! For the projects in this book, you only need a straight stitch and a zigzag stitch, but it's nice to play around with some fancy stitches! Read your manual and be sure your machine is threaded correctly. A badly threaded machine is often responsible for dodgy sewing. If you don't have a manual, they are often available online. If you don't have a machine, it's not the end of the world – you can still sew things (just more slowly!), using running stitch and backstitch.

Straight pins

These are just ordinary dressmaker's pins. Buy good-quality pins, as they will be sharper and finer. I sew right over my pins, although I flinch when I do, and have never broken a needle. Lots of experts warn against this, so go carefully and see if your sewing machine likes pins (have a spare sewing machine needle on standby). It's very good to have a pincushion to store your pins.

Tailor's chalk

Tailor's or dressmaker's chalk is for making temporary marks on the wrong side of fabric. It will brush off with a toothbrush and cold water. I tend to use my air-fading marker instead of tailor's chalk, but see what suits you!

Transfer pencil

A great tool for embroidery. Draw or trace your embroidery design with a transfer pencil, then flip the drawing over and iron it onto your fabric with a hot iron. Remember your design will be reversed.

Transferring an embroidery design onto fabric

Tracing the design

Have a look at our Tote Bag project on page 42 for more on this technique. Take your fabric piece and design. This could be a drawing you've done, a designs from this book, something you've printed off, or a page from a colouring book. Tape your original, right side up, to a well-lit and clean window. Be sure it's straight. Tape your fabric, right side out, over the top of the design, checking you've placed it in the right spot on your fabric. Then trace it. If you're going to embroider it straight away, you can use an air-fading marker to trace it – but be hasty, or you'll need to be re-tracey! Or you can buy special carbon paper for embroidery that will allow you to trace your design onto darker fabrics. Position the paper between your right-side-up fabric and your design and draw carefully over the design to transfer it.

Transferring the design

You can buy a transfer pencil from sewing stores or online. These are great as you just trace over all the lines on your design, pin the piece of paper right side down onto your right-side-up fabric and press firmly with a medium–hot iron to transfer. Remember your design will appear in reverse, so you'll need to reverse your image if that matters. And reverse any text, because it's very hard to read backwards!

Water-soluble marker

A type of sewing pen that wipes off with cold water. Always buy a reputable brand when purchasing marking pens as sometimes the cheaper ones don't work properly and don't wash out!

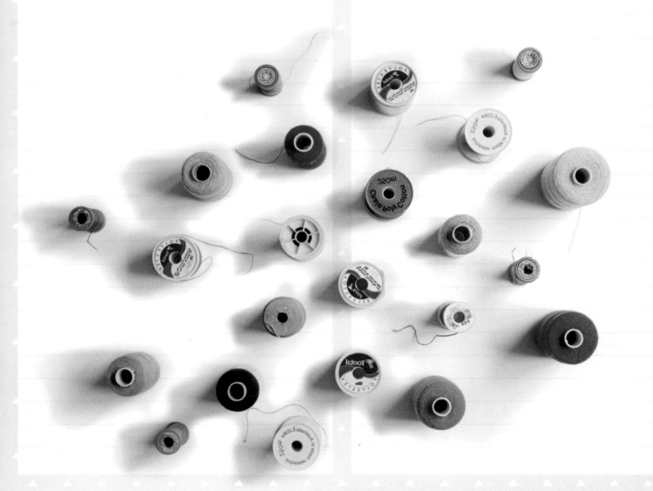

How to knit

Oh, knitting! Knitting was my first yarny foray into the world of craft. My nanna was a really super-dooper expert knitter. She would knit in front of the TV, producing gorgeous things without ever looking away from this week's episode of *Hart to Hart.* As with most crafty endeavours, becoming a whizz requires lots of practice, and there is no time like the present to start working on your technique. Off you go! Knit on!

Knitting tips

Your pattern will tell you which needles and yarn to use, and the recommended needle size also appears on the label of your yarn. If in doubt, ask your friendly yarn retailer. If you are buying yarn online, the bigger yarn websites have comprehensive guides to yarn, needles and more.

Holding the needles and yarn

Don't worry if you're all fingers and thumbs to start off with – those fingers and thumbs will be your very favourite friends once you get the hang of this. There are lots of ways to hold your needles, but why don't you try holding the right needle in the right hand just like a pencil? Hold the left needle lightly at the top, using your thumb and index finger to control it. Make sure you are comfy and relaxed. Be sure that your yarn is in the right place (at the front

or the back of your work – according to the stitch you are knitting) and that you're not knitting with the 'tail' of your yarn. Look carefully at your work as you knit. Take your time so you can catch any stitches before they drop!

Dye lots

Each ball of yarn comes from a particular dye lot. If you're using more than one ball of yarn for a project, be sure they are all from the same dye lot. The dye lot details appear on the label of the yarn. I always buy a little extra, so I have some back-up yarn in the exact same shade. That way you can be sure that all your yarn matches nicely.

Tension

Tension is not a bad thing in knitting. It's a really good thing, and it's really good to get a handle on your tension, so to speak. Relax your hands and wrists and even tension will come a little more naturally. Some patterns will recommend you knit a square to work out whether your tension is tight or loose – which will mean your project might end up bigger or smaller than intended. Check your pattern – it will have a little note about how many stitches should fit into a certain number of centimetres or inches. Measure your work and adjust your knitting accordingly – if it's too small, loosen up a bit, or too big, tighten up those stitches! If you just can't make your stitches any tighter or looser, then change needles to get the right tension. If, when you measure your work, you've got more stitches than the pattern says, change to needles a size larger. Fewer stitches than the pattern says? Change to needles a size smaller. Knit another sample and measure it again to see if it's turned out right. Have a look on the internet – it is full of how-to-knit videos, in case you need to see all this in action.

How to cast on

Make a not-too-tight slip knot and put it on your left-hand needle (for instructions on how to tie a slip knot, see How to Crochet on page 138).

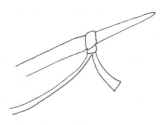

Poke the right-hand knitting needle into the slip knot (you should poke from front to back to make an 'X' with your needles). Now wrap the yarn (make sure it's the ball end – not the tail of the yarn) around the point of the right-hand needle. You should wrap the yarn by taking it under then back over the right-hand needle; the yarn should be lying between the two needles.

Keep the yarn pulled fairly tightly in your right hand. Carefully sliding the right-hand needle down, poke the tip of it down and through the stitch on the left-hand needle. You should now have two loops – one on each needle.

Poke the left-hand needle into the loop on the right-hand needle and transfer this loop over to the left one. Pull your yarn firmly but not tightly. That's a cast on! You'll have two on your left needle now.

Let's make another stitch! Poke the right-hand needle into the top loop on the left-hand needle. We're going to do it all again! Wrap the yarn around the right-hand needle as before (from front to back). Then, as before, poke the tip of the right-hand needle down and through the top stitch on the left-hand needle. You'll now have two stitches on the left needle and one on the right. Transfer this right loop, or stitch, over to the left-hand needle to join the other 'cast-on' stitches. Continue on like this until the required number of stitches is cast on. Note that your original slip stitch counts as one cast-on stitch.

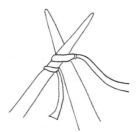

Basic knit stitch

A bumpy stitch that my nan calls 'plain' stitch. It's also referred to as 'garter stitch'. Start with your cast-on stitches on the left needle. The strand of yarn leading to the ball of yarn should be at the back of your work. Now insert the right needle into the top stitch on the left needle as shown. The right needle needs to be tucked in behind the left one to form an 'X' – the left needle is at the front with its little row of 'cast-on' stitches. See?

Wrap the yarn around and over the point of the right-hand needle (which should still be tucked behind and at the rear of the left one). Keep the yarn fairly tight.

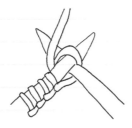

Slide the right-hand needle downwards carefully and poke the point of the right-hand needle down and under the top stitch on the left needle. Now you just slip the top stitch on the left needle off the left needle. There you go, you knitted a stitch. Hurrah!

Basic purl stitch

For purl stitch, start with your cast-on stitches on the left needle (in your left hand). The yarn attached to the ball should be at the front of your work. Now insert the right needle into the top stitch on the left needle as shown. The right needle should be at the front. (The left needle is tucked behind at the rear to form an 'X'. It's kind of the opposite of the basic knit stitch.)

Wrap the yarn over the front and then around under the tip of the right needle to create a loop. Excellent.

Carefully slide the right-hand needle downwards and under the left-hand needle. Slip the top loop off the left-hand needle to complete the stitch. Awesome, you purled!

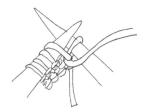

How to cast off [bind off]

This is how you finish off your knitting when you are at the last row. It creates a nice finished edge and stops your knitting from unravelling.

Loosely knit the first two stitches using the basic knit stitch. How funny, but you need two stitches on your right needle to cast off one stitch. You will now have your nearly finished work on the left needle and two stitches on the right needle.

Using either the tip of the left needle, if you are dextrous, or your fingers if you are not, pull the bottom loop up and over the top loop. Now you should have only one stitch on the right needle. Knit the next stitch (from the left needle with your nearly finished work on it). Now again pull the bottom loop up and over the top loop and off the needle. Continue on like this until you have cast off [bound off] all but one stitch.

Thread the 'tail' of the yarn through this last stitch and tie off securely. Voila!

It's a good idea to cast off loosely so that the edge of your knitting is not too tight. This is especially important when you're knitting something with a hem or cuffs, such as a jumper [sweater] – you want to be able to get it on and off easily! If you find it difficult to slip one stitch over another when you're casting off, you can replace the right-hand needle with a crochet hook of a similar thickness. That should make it easier to hook the stitches and cast them off.

How to crochet

Oh my gosh. If everyone learned to crochet the world would be a woolly, happy place. I love to crochet. It is my favourite craft of all. I have only been crocheting for a few short years, and when I was learning I cried. In frustration. A lot. I was THAT desperate to be good at it, and with persistence and lots of hours with a hook and some crochet videos I got there. I do not recommend crying, but I do recommend the persistence and practice. I want you to crochet, I really do. You will LOVE it once you get the knack of it. Please do try. Go on!

Slip knot

The slip knot is the very first stitch you slip onto your crochet hook! Here's how to slip!

> Place the yarn over your finger like so. Be sure you have plenty of excess.

> Wrap the excess yarn around your fingertip two more times.

> Now pull Loop A up and over Loop B as shown.

> Next, you need to pull Loop B up and over Loop A.

> Now grab the Back Loop and pull it up and off your finger – you'll be dragging the other loop after it, thus making a slip knot.

> Voila!

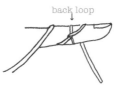

Simple slip stitch

The slip stitch is often used to anchor or gather in your work as you crochet. We use it in all the crochet projects in this book.

   With the loop still on your hook, push the hook through the last stitch of your work as specified. Hook your yarn over the hook and pull this new loop through to the front of your work and through the bottom two loops on your hook.

Chain stitch

Chain stitch is often the foundation for crochet projects. Granny squares, granny stripes and simple rounds can all start with the humble chain. Practise by making lovely long chains and then get into some proper projects.

> Put your slip knot onto the hook – we'll call it Loop A.

> Wrap your yarn around the hook like so:

> Hook the just-wrapped-around yarn B under Loop A to make your very first chain.

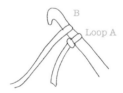

> It should look a bit like this:

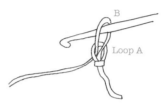

> Make another chain. Wrap your yarn around, then hook yarn C under Loop B as shown:

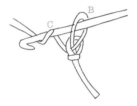

> You've made another chain – hurrah!

> Continue on in this manner – making as many chain stitches as you need to. Note that your original slip stitch does NOT count as one chain.

Double crochet
(referred to as single crochet in the US)

A simple neat stitch that makes a nice firm solid crochet 'fabric'. If you are looking for a sturdy, simple stitch, DC [SC] is it!

> With the loop on your hook, push your hook into the front of the second chain stitch from your hook. You don't count the stitch on your hook, though. Start on the next one.

> With your hook still pushed through that stitch, hook your yarn and pull it back through to the front of your work. You should now have two loops on the hook.

> Hook your yarn again and pull this hooked yarn under the bottom two loops on your hook.

> You should now have one loop on your hook again.

> Hook into the next chain across and repeat.

> When you reach the end of a row, turn your work around, chain up one and continue on.

Treble crochet
(referred to as double crochet in the US)

I like treble stitch [double crochet], because it's a vital stitch in the world of granny squaring! When you crochet a granny square, you treble [double crochet] these stitches in and out of a foundation circle or loop. But crochet is not just about grannies, is it? You can also treble stitch [double crochet] into a length of chain stitch for less granny-type projects.

> With the loop on your hook, push your hook through your chosen stitch (or ring or gap, depending on your project). For many projects this will be the third chain stitch from the hook. But, if you're making a granny square, then you should hook into the 'gap or ring' as detailed in your instructions.

> With the hook still pushed through, hook your yarn and pull it back through to the front of your work.

> Now you need to hook your yarn around yet again. You'll now have four loops on your hook.

> Next, pull the loop near the hooky tip under and through the middle two loops – leaving you with only two loops on your hook (not four anymore).

> Now hook your yarn around again and pull it through the bottom two loops. You should now have only one loop on your hook. Yippee!

> Repeat as detailed in your instructions.

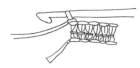

Note: If you're crocheting a row rather than a granny square, when you get to the end of your row, turn your work around. Chain stitch up three and continue on.

Crochet abbreviations and terms

These vary dramatically. This book uses the UK, Australian and international terminology, with the North American term in square brackets.

Abbreviation	UK, Australian and international term
ch	chain
sl st	slip stitch
dc	double crochet (referred to as single crochet [SC] in North America)
tr	treble (referred to as double crochet [DC] in North America)
(s)	stitches

Note on hooks

There are recommended hook sizes for various thicknesses of yarn. Consult your yarn store for advice, as it really does make a huge difference to the finished size and result of your project. The correct hook with the correct yarn will give you the very best result.

Note on yarn

Always use the yarn thickness (ply) recommended – many projects simply won't work if you use the wrong ply, although experienced crocheters can often juggle yarns and hooks and gauge and make it work. Once you learn the basics you can cut loose and freestyle it a bit, like the experts!

Holiday reading list

Reading. It is very important to read, especially on a holiday or a sunny day or a day with the letter 'y' in it. Do not say you are too busy to read. You are never too busy to read, and even FIVE teensy minutes a day will open your mind to all sorts of possibilities and imaginings not available to us in the 'real' world. Here is a list of extra favourite classic books to read. I asked all my friends and favourite people what they liked and then added my own to round it all off nicely. Please read. Even for a teensy minute. You deserve it!

1. Great Expectations: Charles Dickens
2. A Tale of Two Cities: Charles Dickens
3. Oliver Twist: Charles Dickens
4. David Copperfield: Charles Dickens
5. My Family and Other Animals: Gerald Durrell
6. The Way We Live Now: Anthony Trollope
7. Doctor Wartle's School: Anthony Trollope
8. He Knew He Was Right: Anthony Trollope
9. Cousin Henry: Anthony Trollope
10. Emma: Jane Austen
11. Persuasion: Jane Austen
12. Mansfield Park: Jane Austen
13. Pride and Prejudice: Jane Austen
14. Sense and Sensibility: Jane Austen
15. Cranford: Elizabeth Gaskell
16. North and South: Elizabeth Gaskell
17. Stiff Upper Lip, Jeeves: P G Wodehouse
18. Little Women: Louisa May Alcott
19. Little Men: Louisa May Alcott
20. An Old-fashioned Girl: Louisa May Alcott
21. Wuthering Heights: Emily Bronte
22. The Tenant of Wildfell Hall: Anne Bronte
23. Agnes Grey: Anne Bronte
24. Jane Eyre: Charlotte Bronte
25. Villette: Charlotte Bronte
26. Alice's Adventures in Wonderland: Lewis Carroll
27. Winesburg Ohio: Sherwood Anderson
28. The Great Gatsby: F Scott Fitzgerald
29. Washington Square: Henry James
30. The Age of Innocence: Edith Wharton
31. The Custom of the Country: Edith Wharton
32. The House of Mirth: Edith Wharton
33. Madame Bovary: Gustave Flaubert
34. Wide Sargasso Sea: Jean Rhys
35. Middlemarch: George Eliot
36. East of Eden: John Steinbeck
37. Dracula: Bram Stoker
38. Frankenstein: Mary Shelley
39. On the Side of the Angels: Betty Miller
40. Farewell Leicester Square: Betty Miller
41. Monochromes: Ella D'Arcy
42. Modern Instances: Ella D'Arcy
43. Crossrigs: Jane and Mary Findlater
44. Adam Bede: George Elliot
45. Love in a Fallen City: Eileen Chang
46. Lust, Caution: Eileen Chang
47. Anna Karenina: Leo Tolstoy
48. Charlie and the Chocolate Factory: Roald Dahl
49. A Tree Grows in Brooklyn: Betty Smith
50. The Count of Monte Cristo: Alexandre Dumas
51. The End of the Affair: Graham Greene
52. The Diary of a Young Girl: Anne Frank
53. Miss Pettigrew Lives for a Day: Winifred Watson
54. Tess of the D'Urbervilles: Thomas Hardy
55. To Kill a Mockingbird: Harper Lee
56. The Eagle of the Ninth: Rosemary Sutcliff
57. The Master and Margarita: Mikhail Bulgakov
58. The Woman in White: Wilkie Collins
59. Wind in the Willows: Kenneth Grahame
60. The Picture of Dorian Gray: Oscar Wilde
61. Love in a Cold Climate: Nancy Mitford
62. The Pursuit of Love: Nancy Mitford
63. Rebecca: Daphne du Maurier
64. My Brilliant Career: Miles Franklin
65. Anne of Green Gables: L M Montgomery
66. The Blue Castle: L M Montgomery
67. Lord of the Flies: William Golding
68. The Sound and the Fury: William Faulkner
69. As I Lay Dying: William Faulkner
70. To the Lighthouse: Virginia Woolf
71. Bel Ami: Guy de Maupassant
72. Of Human Bondage: W Somerset Maugham
73. Love in the Time of Cholera: Gabriel Garcia Marquez
74. Ender's Game: Orson Scott Card
75. Gulliver's Travels: Jonathan Swift
76. Moby Dick: Herman Melville
77. The Adventures of Huckleberry Finn: Mark Twain
78. Don Quixote: Miguel de Cervantes
79. The Bell Jar: Sylvia Plath
80. Catcher in the Rye: J D Salinger
81. The Outsiders: S E Hinton
82. Brideshead Revisited: Evelyn Waugh
83. Cold Comfort Farm: Stella Gibbons
84. The Old Man and the Sea: Ernest Hemingway
85. Lady Chatterley's Lover: D H Lawrence
86. On the Road: Jack Kerouac
87. All Quiet on the Western Front: Erich Maria Remarque
88. Little Birds: Anais Nin
89. The Plague: Albert Camus
90. Catch-22: Joseph Heller

Steve's sunshine playlist

PROPERTY OF
CONNETQUOT SCHOOLS
C.S.D. #7

Always The Sun » Stranglers
King Of The Beach » Wavves
Let's Go Surfing » The Drums
Someone Somewhere In Summertime
  » Simple Minds
Vacation » Beach Fossils
Summertime » The Sundays
Summer Holiday » Wild Nothing
Good Vibrations » The Beachboys
Crazy For You » Best Coast
Sunny » Georgie Fame And The Blue Flames
Sunshine Smile » Adorable
Deep Hit Of Morning Sun » Primal Scream
Close Your Eyes » Dot Allison
Long Hot Summer » The Style Council
Chewing Gum » Annie
Rocket Summer » The Afternoons
Summer Jets » Iain Archer

Vapour Trail » Ride
Don't Fear » Maps
Pure » Lightning Seeds
Rise And Shine » Cardigans
Mr Tambourine Man » The Byrds
Summertime Clothes » Animal Collective
Don't Look Back Into The Sun » The Libertines
Indian Summer » Beat Happening
Celestica » Crystal Castles
Young Folks » Peter Bjorn and John
Jump In The Pool » Friendly Fires
Triangle Cloud » Gold Panda
Here Comes The Sun » The Beatles
Aint That Enough? » Teenage Fanclub
Up Up And Away » The 5th Dimension
Makes No Sense At All » Husker Du
Swim » Surfer Blood
Love Like A Sunset » Phoenix

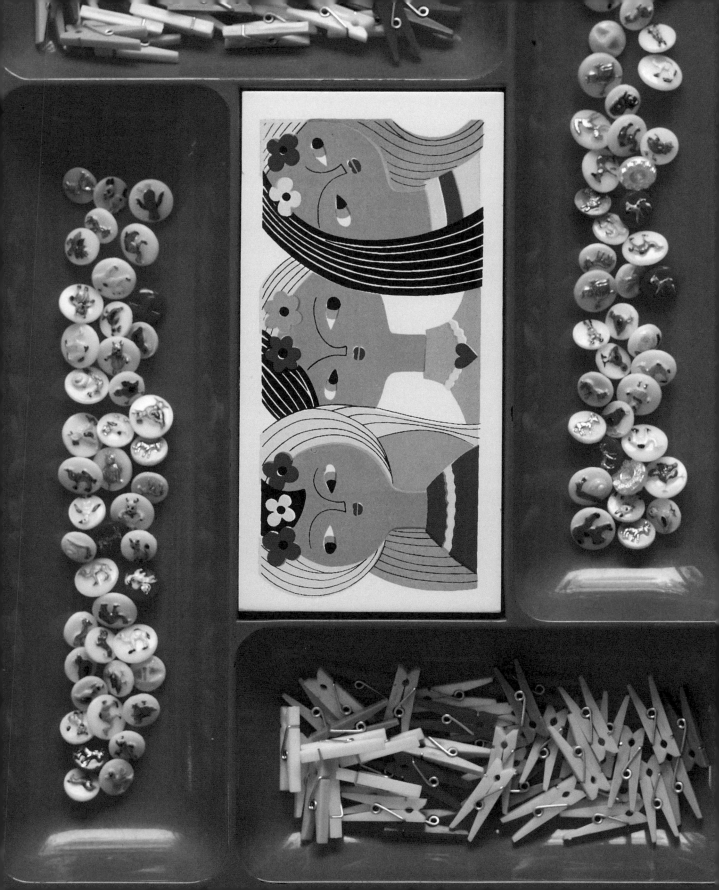

Inspirations

Upon a Fold
uponafold.com.au

At Swim-Two-Birds
at-swim-two-birds.blogspot.com

Whipup
whipup.net

Famille Summerbelle
famillesummerbelle.com

Fryd + Design
frydogdesign.blogspot.com

And Now I Am Broke
andnowiambroke.blogspot.com

Fine Little Day
finelittleday.com

Emma Lamb
emmallamb.blogspot.com

Dos Family
dosfamily.com

Bricolagelife
bricolagelife.typepad.com

The Selby
theselby.com

Pirouette
pirouetteblog.com

Hello, I'm Tiger
hello-tiger.blogspot.com

Michelle Mackintosh
michellemackintosh.tumblr.com

Smitten Kitchen
smittenkitten.com.au

Poppytalk
poppytalk.blogspot.com

Attic24
attic24.typepad.com

Beci Orpin
beciorpin.com

Mieke Willems
miekewillems.blogspot.com

Decor8
decor8blog.com

Posie Gets Cozy
rosylittlethings.typepad.com

Gemma Jones
gemmajones.net

Pickles
pickle.no

Frankie
frankie.com.au

Lotta Jansdotter
jansdotter.com

Dottie Angel
dottieangel.blogspot.com

Amy Karol
amykarol.com

Wood & Wool Stool
woodwoolstool.blogspot.com

Rose Hip
rosehip.typepad.com

Three Buttons
threebuttons.blogspot.com

Milk Magazine
milkmagazine.net

Modern Kiddo
modernkiddo.com

Things we were watching

It is a very important skill to be able to watch quality television while making things. It was taught to me by my nanna, who crocheted in front of *MacGyver*, *Hart to Hart* and *Fantasy Island*. I would like to pass this skill to you, dear reader. Here are the productions that fuelled this book. Maybe you could add your own to the list?

Little Dorrit
Spicks and Specks
Outnumbered
Enid
Miss Potter
The Moonstone
Bed of Roses
Tenko

The Tenant of Wildfell Hall
Cold Comfort Farm
Born and Bred
The Real Housewives of Most Places
Sarah Wiener and the Kitchen Kids
The King's Speech
Breaking Bad

Downton Abbey
Boardwalk Empire
Big Love
Sense and Sensibility
Grey Gardens
My Family And Other Animals
Lorna Doone
Persuasion

Vanity Fair
Cranford
Pride and Prejudice
Upstairs Downstairs
Mapp and Lucia
Paper Giants
Lost in Austen
Jane Eyre

Acknowledgements

Thank you to these lovely people.

> My excellent family: Cam, Max, Rin and Ari

> My excellent family part 2: Sara and Mason
  and Andy, Mum and Sean and Nan and Ken too

> To Gemma and Anita: Smooches to the best
  pals a gal can have

> Thank you Bronte

> Michelle and Steve: my favourite couple

> To Kirsty: for being a bud and for the lovely
  stitch guide she made for this book

> To the Chez Ladies: Victoria, Cass, Bec, Myf
  and Susie

> And the Ladies of the Night: Olivia, Beci, Nat,
  Lou, Shelley and Fiona

> And to the Ladies of Rad: Anna B, Rayna,
  Angela, Emma, Molly, Aimee, Sass and Sue

> To the super-fave Dave Gray, Andre and Lulu

> Jane Winning: who is the best editor a gal
  could hope for and just the best gal, full stop

> Janine Flew: The craft detective

> John Laurie and Chris Middleton: For the
  photos! I thank you!

> To everyone at Hardie Grant for making such
  beautiful books

> Fliss: for bringing the beautiful Betsy along to
  our shoot!

> Tim Collins at Cloud: for lending us your lovely
  Realax stools

> Sonia Post: for lending us your lovely things
  for our photoshoot.

> Marieke and Michaela for being hot and smart

> Mr Ghostpatrol and Miss Miso for being really
  nice neighbours

> Fee and Jess and Ben and Michelle B for letting
  me on the radio sometimes and for being rad

> *Frankie* and 3RRR and Outre Gallery and
  Captains of Industry

> The very crafty and sweet Brown Owls peeps

> All our Mike's customers, past and present

> My other favourite kids: Isabella, Leroy, Leo,
  Hazel, Luka, Royce

> The really lovely people who take the time to
  read my blog and support the things I do

> The internet for helping me make nice friends

> The Real Housewives of Orange County, New
  Jersey, New York, Miami, DC, Beverly Hills
  and Atlanta for keeping me company during
  the crochet

> The Hendrickson Family for entertaining me
  during the embroidery

> And of course huge thanks to all at *Downton
  Abbey*

> To my fellow bloggers, crafty and not, for being
  such great online neighbours

> To Dur-e and David. And to Nellie and her
  team, too

Published in 2011 by
Hardie Grant Books

Hardie Grant Books (Australia)
Ground Floor, Building 1
658 Church Street
Richmond, Victoria 3121
www.hardiegrant.com.au

Hardie Grant Books (UK)
Second Floor, North Suite
Dudley House
Southampton Street
London WC2E 7HF
www.hardiegrant.co.uk

Cataloguing-in-Publication data is available from the National Library of Australia.

ISBN 978 1 74270 131 8

Publisher: Paul McNally
Project editor: Jane Winning
Design, layout, styling and pattern illustrations: Michelle Mackintosh
Additional styling: Pip Lincolne
Photography: John Laurie
Food preparation: Toula Ploumidis
Copy editing: Janine Flew
Colour reproduction by Splitting Image Colour Studio
Printed in China by 1010 Printing International Limited

The publisher would like to thank Michelle Mackintosh and Steve Wide for their generosity in lending their beautiful house to make this book.

Thanks also to the following companies for fabrics and crafty supplies: RJR Fabrics (Kitten PlayDate fabric by Thimbleberries in Huckleberry Bottle Totes), Rowan Fabrics (Foxgloves fabric in Sweet Ride Bike Seat Cover), Spotlight (various fabrics in Friendly Blankets for Cosy Couples), Lincraft (blank tote in Chatty Tote), Deans Art (e-z cut carving medium in Amazingly Cute Gift Bags and porcelain markers in Ceramic DIY-namic).